A New Slant on Bargello Quilts

Marge Edie

Martingale
& COMPANY

Acknowledgments

I might have never started exploring the many geometries possible with Bargello if my husband, Dan, had not said, "Since you like to do puzzles so much, why don't you take some computer programming classes?" back in 1978. That question, and my return to the Clemson University campus, changed my life.

But before that, I must thank my father, who encouraged me to love math with the "Number Facts" games we would play in spare moments when I was just a little girl. He'd throw out all kinds of problems for me to do in my head and would then check my answer after a stream of multiplication and division exercises. I also remember, with respect, the demanding Mr. Wade and Mr. May—algebra and geometry teachers in Muskogee, Oklahoma, and Colerain High School in Cincinnati, Ohio—who wanted desperately for their students to put their brains in gear and finally grasp the concepts.

Thanks to Dan again for his willingness to put up with my need to "make things." He is my best advisor, critic, and supporter. And to my mother who thinks anything I make is wonderful! I also want to acknowledge the stimulating group of quilters who respond and react to what I create and share their own beautiful work with me. These exciting interactions spur me on to produce more, and hopefully better, fabric art. Specifically, thanks to my friends in our Upstate of South Carolina Focus art quilt group. The monthly critique days are invaluable and keep us all on track.

In particular, I want to thank Priscilla Evans Hair and Susan Kopczyk for being willing to experiment with new Bargello ideas on their own, and Ann Hawkins, Lori Kuba, and Gale Pemberton, for contributing their talents for the gallery in this book.

To all my friends and colleagues at Martingale & Company—especially my editor, Christine Barnes—thanks for your time and patience in helping me convey my geometric images to the quilting world.

Without the support of all these friends and loved ones, this book would never have happened.

Credits

Technical Editor .... Christine Barnes
Copy Editor .... Tina Cook
Design and Production Manager .... Cheryl Stevenson
Cover Designer .... Lisa Robinson
Text Designer .... Kay Green
Illustrator .... Robin Strobel
Photographer .... Brent Kane

A New Slant on Bargello Quilts
© 1998 by Marge Edie
Martingale & Company
PO Box 118
Bothell, WA 98041-0118 USA

Printed in Hong Kong
03 02 01 00 99 98   6 5 4 3 2 1

Library of Congress Cataloging-in-Publication Data
Edie, Marge
      A new slant on Bargello quilts / Marge Edie.
         p. cm.
      ISBN 1-56477-227-6
      1. Patchwork—Patterns. 2. Strip quilting—Patterns.
3. Patchwork quilts. I. Title.
TT835.E377 1998
746.46'041—dc21   98-4510
                                                             CIP

CONTENTS

Introduction -------------- 4

Definitions -------------- 4

Tools ------------------ 5

Bargello Design Paper ------ 7

Fabric Selection ---------- 10

Bargello Basics ---------- 10

Preparing the Fabric ----------- 10

Making Straight Color Runs ------ 11

Making Straight Tubes ---------- 13

Making Slant Color Runs -------- 14

Making Slant Tubes ------------ 16

Pattern Direction -------------- 17

Creating the Curve ------------- 18

Making a Paper Graph ---------- 19

Preparing the Backing
   and Batting ---------------- 20

Cutting Tubes into Loops --------- 21

Arranging Loops on
   Your Design Wall ------------ 22

Opening Loops to
   Make Bargello Strips --------- 22

Stitching Bargello Strips --------- 23

Borders and Binding ------- 25

Adding Borders --------------- 26

Binding Your Quilt ------------- 27

Troubleshooting ----------- 29

Connecting Upward and
   Downward Curves — 30

Using Color Changes
   to Create Dimension— 31

Floating a Design on
   a Plain Background — 32

Patterns ---------------- 32

Vermont --------------------- 33

Tidal Pool -------------------- 40

Radiance --------------------- 46

Year of the Dragon ------------- 55

Vail ----------------------- 63

Covenant --------------------- 68

St. Elmo's Fire ---------------- 75

Crystal City -------------------- 81

Gallery ---------------- 88

Meet the Author ---------- 96

INTRODUCTION

Beyond the geometries of traditional Bargello lies another world of related designs that incorporate strips with a 45° slant. Combining slant Bargello strips with straight Bargello strips, or using slant strips alone, creates new, dynamic Bargello structures that are still fast and relatively simple to make. Whether the designs are formal and elegant, with determined strip relationships, or freer, with loose geometric connections between the elements, the result is powerful and exciting.

The creation of the Bias Stripper™ ruler by Donna Lynn Thomas makes the measurement of slanted strips virtually automatic. So thank you, Donna, for making our quilting jobs a lot easier! I was in the process of trying to invent the same tool, to market in conjunction with this book, when Donna's ruler emerged to be used with her book *Stripples* (That Patchwork Place, 1995). Once you become familiar with this ruler's uses, you will discover many ways to streamline other piecing projects.

In this book, you will learn to make beautiful Bargello quilts using strips that have a built-in slant. These strips are cut from tubes specially constructed, with help from the Bias Stripper, for slant designs. Some of the projects are made with only slant strips, while others combine slant strips with straight ones. "Vermont," while it uses both slant and straight Bargello strips, demands no matching of seams and is a great beginner project. Others, like "Vail," are a bit more advanced and require more precision. The more complex quilts explore a wide range of Bargello possibilities, while inspiring the quilt artist to develop original designs. Graph and Bargello-strip paper are included on pages 7–9 for those who wish to experiment.

As with any quilt structure, color and contrast within the work help create its beauty. These quilt projects, since they take relatively little time, offer the quilter the opportunity to experiment and develop in the areas of color and design. The creative possibilities are endless!

DEFINITIONS

Many of these terms will be familiar to quilters who have made Bargello quilts from my first book. A few new terms are necessary for slant Bargello.

Color-Run Strips: Individual strips of fabric that make up a color run. Color-run strips may be cut straight, from selvage to selvage, or on a 45° slant.

Color Run: Strips of fabric sewn together to make a rectangle, called a straight color run, or a parallelogram, called a slant color run. Slant color runs may slant up or down.

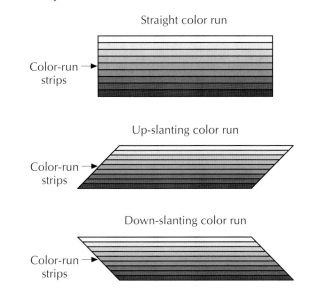

Tube: One or more color runs sewn together to form a continuous tube of fabric. Tubes may be straight, up-slanting, or down-slanting.

Loops: Strips cut from a straight or a slant tube.

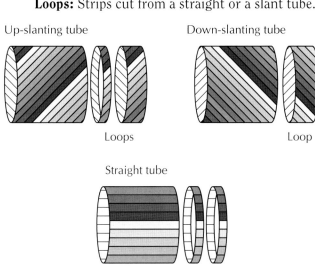

Bargello Strips: Strips cut from color runs, or loops that are opened.

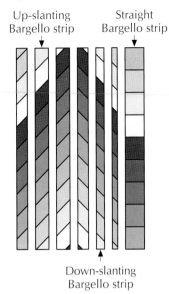

Up-slanting Bargello strip

Straight Bargello strip

Down-slanting Bargello strip

Graphed Curve: A Bargello design chart, indicating the width of the design area, the width of the Bargello strips, how many strips to cut, and whether they will move up or down. The graph does not indicate the width of the color-run strips or whether the Bargello strips will be cut from straight, up-slanting, or down-slanting color runs or tubes.

Blocks: Segments of a graphed curve that represent Bargello strip widths.

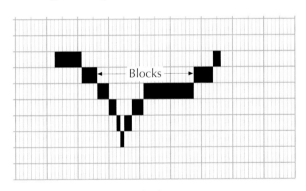

Blocks

Graphed curve

TOOLS

For cutting strips, you will need a rotary cutter with a sharp blade, a large cutting mat, and a 6" x 24" clear acrylic ruler. A 24" x 36" gridded cutting mat is best for these projects.

You will also need the Bias Stripper ruler, from Martingale & Company, to cut the narrower strips for slant color-run strips that match, on the diagonal, corresponding straight color-run strips.

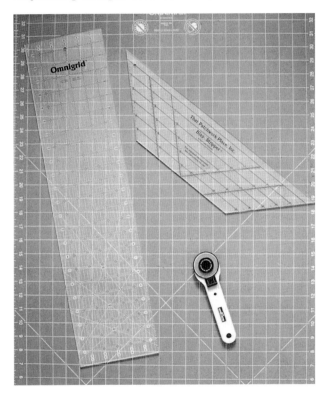

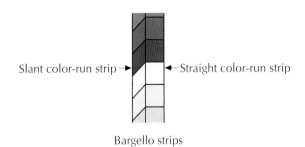

Slant color-run strip → ← Straight color-run strip

Bargello strips

This wonderful tool eliminates the need for complex calculations and measurements when making quilts that contain straight and slant Bargello strips. The measurements on the ruler are approximately 70% of the corresponding measurements on a standard ruler. For example, the 1" measurement on the Bias Stripper actually measures just under ¾". Notice that ½" is built into the ruler for seam allowances, so that every time you make a cut, it includes the two ¼" seam allowances.

Because the seam allowances are included in strips cut with the Bias Stripper, you must base your cuts on the *finished width* of the corresponding straight strip. If, for example, you want to create slant strips that match 3" finished strips cut from a standard quilter's ruler, you must cut the slant strips on the 3" line, not the 3½" line. This method can take some getting used to, but the Bias Stripper is a great addition to any quilter's tools.

Your sewing machine is essential for this quilt-as-you-build-it work. Make sure it has reliable tension control and that the presser foot does not push down too firmly onto the fabric and batting. Otherwise, the presser foot will push your Bargello strips forward as you sew them.

Also have on hand a seam ripper. To make sewing corrections easiest, set your machine's stitch length to about ten stitches per inch and relax your thread tension just enough to make ripping out possible.

These projects require a lot of pinning. Long, straight pins with round heads prevent wear and tear on your fingertips. You will also need fabric shears, thread-snipping scissors, safety pins, thread to generally match the fabrics in your color runs, and bobbin thread to match the backing. A reducing glass or Ruby Beholder™ is great for determining the proper arrangement of your fabrics for the best contrast.

If you want to design your own slant Bargello quilt, photocopy the graph paper on the following page. To draw your own curve, you will need a No. 2 pencil, an eraser, and transparent tape. Use a ballpoint pen or felt-tip marker to check off the blocks on the graph as you complete them.

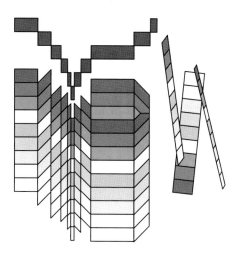

Photocopy the Bargello strip paper on pages 8 and 9 to practice your slant design before committing fabric to a quilt. With your rotary equipment and an old blade, cut a variety of strips and arrange them in various ways on a photocopy of the graph paper. Use a gluestick or transparent tape to attach paper strips to your design as you develop it.

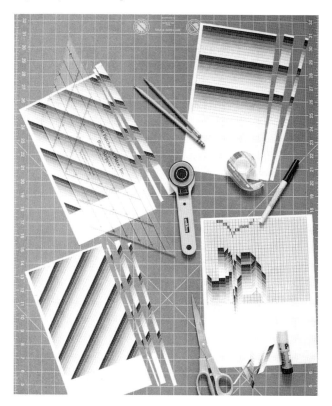

Bargello Graph Paper

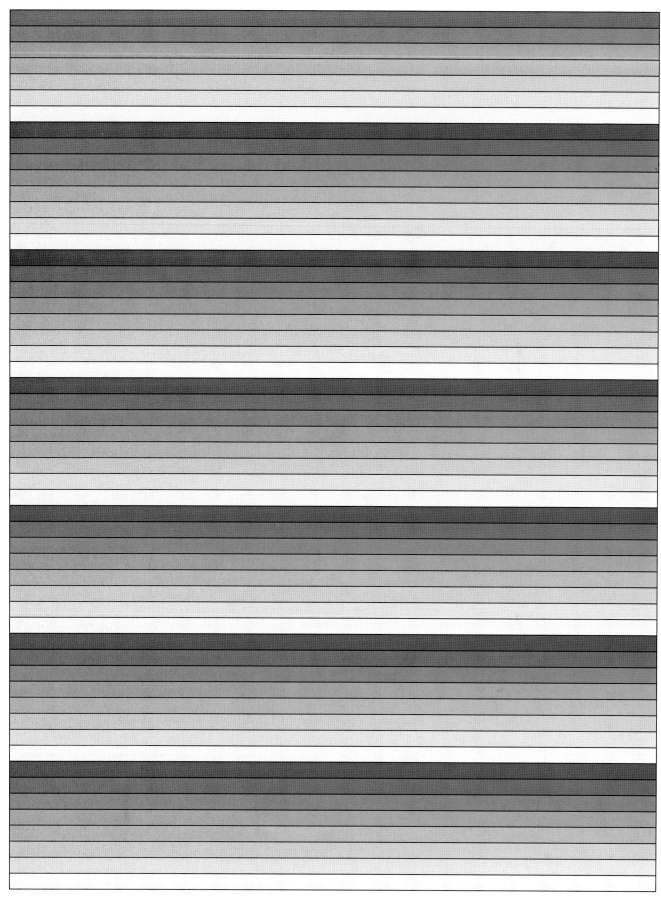

Straight Bargello Strip Paper

Up-slanting Bargello Strip Paper   Down-slanting Bargello Strip Paper

Fabric Selection

The dramatic movement in Bargello quilts is the result of a range of light-to-dark fabrics. Let your instincts guide you in combining interesting prints and textures. The more varied your patterns and textures, the more your quilts will sparkle.

Start with a favorite fabric and select other fabrics to complete your palette. You might also begin with a painting or photo, then pull fabrics that match and complement its colors. Formal color schemes usually have a consistent range of color intensity or brilliance. For excitement, incorporate varied intensities, patterns, textures, and colors. Be sure to choose a variety of values, ranging from light to dark. I avoid solid colors because every imperfection shows!

Although your fabrics may work well together in a variety of ways, I recommend arranging them from dark to light. Your geometries will be at their most dramatic and stunning.

You have the option of cutting your color-run strips straight, from selvage to selvage, or on the diagonal. Either way, you will have to deal with some bias effects. I am willing to mix fine pima cotton, wonderful wax batiks, and low-grade, coarsely woven cheap fabric from the discount house if I like the blend of color and pattern. But I must be very careful in my sewing and pressing to keep the loose weaves from stretching more than the finer fabrics. Bias problems can be nearly eliminated by choosing tightly woven fabrics with a high thread count.

Bargello Basics

Many of the steps required to produce a beautiful slant Bargello quilt are similar to those in traditional Bargello work. These similarities make it possible to combine straight and slant strips for striking designs.

Some of the projects in the book use only slant Bargello strips, while others use a combination of straight and slant Bargello strips. In some cases, you sew the color runs into tubes, cut the tubes into loops, then open the loops to make Bargello strips. For other patterns, you cut the color runs into Bargello strips. Check the patterns (pages 33–87) to see which of the following steps pertain to the quilt you plan to make.

Preparing the Fabric

1. Wash and iron your fabric. Check for colorfastness; if the fabric bleeds when rinsed, continue rinsing until the water remains clear.
2. Fold the fabric lengthwise, matching selvages, wrong sides together.

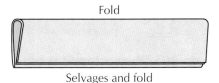

Fold

Selvages

3. Fold the fabric again, matching the first fold line to the selvage edges, creating four thicknesses.

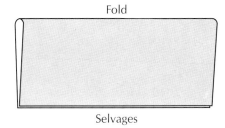

Fold

Selvages and fold

4. For long yardage, accordion pleat each folded length of fabric into a pile that is about 6" x 10½". The fabric will pull easily across the cutting board as you cut strips and will be prefolded when set aside for future use.

Making Straight Color Runs

You make straight color runs using crosswise strips cut from selvage to selvage.

1. Cut the uneven edges off one end of the folded fabric before cutting strips. Align the folded fabric edge with the cutting mat's horizontal lines and align the ruler's lines with the mat's vertical lines. Pressing down firmly on the ruler with your left hand, cut off the ragged edges, pushing the rotary cutter away from you. Reverse this procedure if you are left-handed.

NOTE: *Some people line up the ruler on the other end of the fabric to cut strips. Practice with scrap fabric to see which method you prefer.*

2. To cut strips, place the fabric to the right and measure from the left cut edges. Cut, making sure to cut through all fabric layers.

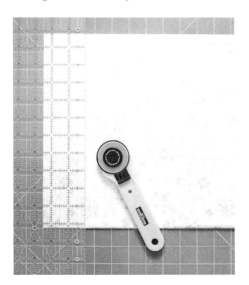

The width of the color run will be the width of the narrowest fabric you use—42" to 45" wide, selvage to selvage. (Fabric widths vary with manufacturers and shrinkage after laundering.)

Tip: Do not cut all the fabric strips to the shortest strip's length. Trim later, after all the strips have been sewn into the tube. If you use one fabric that is much narrower than the other fabrics, cut two or more strips and piece them end to end before sewing the strip into the color run. A seam in one of the color-run strips will not be noticeable.

3. Sew the cut strips together into color runs by chain piecing. To chain-piece, stitch a continuous ¼"-wide seam from strip to strip, without lifting the presser foot or cutting the threads between strips. After you have stitched all the strips of one fabric, clip the threads between units. Turn the color run around and start to sew a new strip at the end of the strip you just finished stitching.

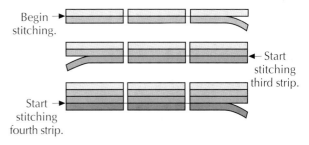

If you keep even-numbered fabric strips on top and odd-numbered strips on the bottom, you will automatically begin stitching each new strip at opposite ends of the color run.

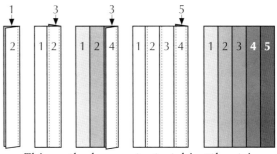

This method prevents stretching the strips as you sew. When successive strips stretch, the color run bows, making it more difficult to cut accurate Bargello strips.

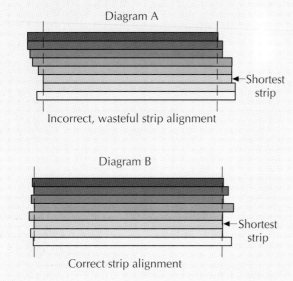

Diagram A

Shortest strip

Incorrect, wasteful strip alignment

Diagram B

Shortest strip

Correct strip alignment

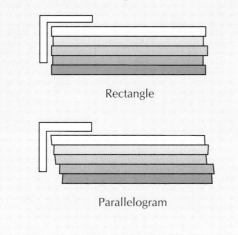

Rectangle

Parallelogram

4. Working on the wrong side of the color run, press the strips toward the lightest fabric. (You press toward the lightest fabric because, when you join the lightest strip to the darkest strip to make the tube, you will naturally press the seam allowances in the same direction, toward the darkest fabric.)

Turn the color run to the right side, reverse your iron, and press in the opposite direction to gently pull and stretch the strips back into shape.

Bowing can also result from improper pressing. If you pull too hard with one hand while pressing, you will stretch and bow the color run.

Making Straight Tubes

Stitching color runs into tubes and cutting loops from the tubes allows you to play with the arrangement of your Bargello strips. Your project's size and design will determine how many color runs make up the tube.

1. To sew one or more color runs into a tube, align the first and last strips, right sides together, and stitch. Press the seam allowances toward the darkest fabric.

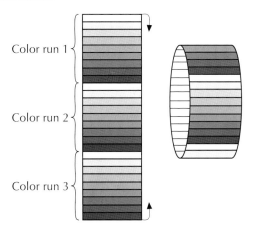

Avoid twisting the color run when sewing it into a tube, or the segments in your Bargello strips will be skewed.

If the tube is too wide to fit on your cutting mat, fold it in half or in thirds lengthwise, creating four or six thicknesses of fabric.

2. Trim the uneven selvages by carefully lining up the folds with the lines on the cutting mat and cutting perpendicular to the folds.

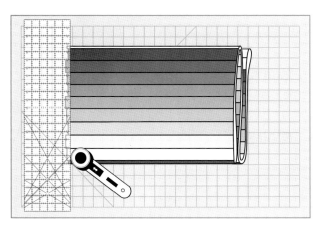

Trimming selvages

3. Using your standard quilter's ruler, cut the loops from the tube according to the Cutting Chart in the pattern directions. If making an original quilt, refer to your graphed design for the width of the loops; remember to add ½" for seam allowances (see "Creating the Curve" on page 18).

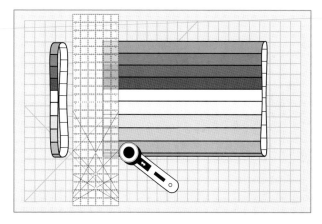

Cutting loops

In some patterns, you cut the color runs into Bargello strips, without making tubes. Check the pattern directions to see how wide to cut the strips. Remember to add ½" for seam allowances.

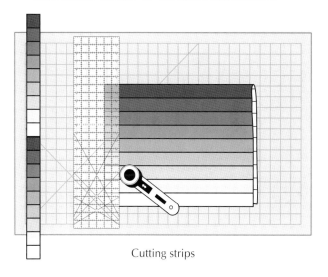

Cutting strips

Making Slant Color Runs

To create Bargello strips that slant up or down, you must first construct slant colors runs. You'll use the Bias Stripper ruler (see pages 5–6) to make slant color runs.

Two ¼" seam allowances in ½" edge.

You can cut strips for slant color runs crosswise, from selvage to selvage, or on the diagonal. Each method has advantages and disadvantages.

For the least waste of fabric, cut your color-run strips for slant tubes from selvage to selvage—just as you would cut strips for straight tubes, except that you will use the Bias Stripper ruler. Strips cut this way will be about 42" long, depending upon the fabric width. If you cut your color-run strips from selvage to selvage, the edges of your *Bargello strips* will be on the bias and will have some stretch. Handle them with care. Fortunately, the process of sewing the Bargello strips onto the backing and batting helps control the stretch.

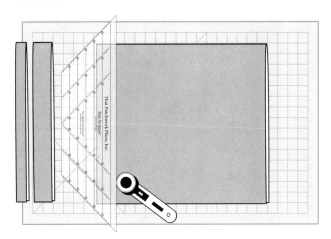

Cutting straight strips

If you cut your color-run strips on the diagonal, the strips will be on the bias, making them more difficult to join. However, when you cut your *Bargello strips,* they will be on the straight grain, minimizing stretch. Another advantage to cutting strips on the diagonal is that they may be longer. Longer strips will result in a tube that is as wide as the corresponding straight tube.

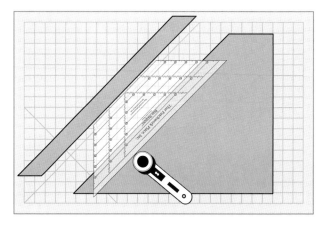

Cutting diagonal strips

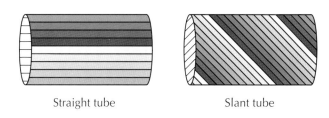

Straight tube   Slant tube

I cut most of my strips for slant color runs from selvage to selvage because it is the most economical use of the fabric. The resulting tube is narrower than a tube made from straight Bargello strips.

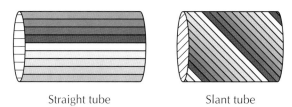

Straight tube   Slant tube

Because there is considerable trimming on the sides of slant color runs and tubes and, therefore, more fabric loss than with straight-tube construction, it's best to create as wide a tube as required for a project. The pattern directions indicate how many fabric strips to piece end to end to make a tube wide enough for the quilt you are making.

1. Read the directions that come with the Bias Stripper ruler before you begin. Using the Bias Stripper, cut the slant color-run strips as indicated in the directions for the quilt you are making. (Remember, this ruler has a built-in ½" for the seam allowances.) If cutting slant strips for an original design in which the slant strips will match straight strips, cut each slant strip as wide as the *finished width* of the corresponding straight strip.

2. To construct a color run for up-slanting Bargello strips, cut each strip as shown below. For down-slanting Bargello strips, cut the color run strip on the opposite diagonal. It's a good idea to stagger the location of the 45° cut so the seams occur randomly in your color runs.

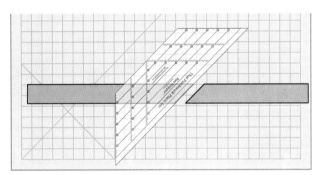

Cut strip for up-slanting Bargello tube

Cut strip for down-slanting Bargello tube

3. Trim the selvages and sew each strip back together at the straight ends.

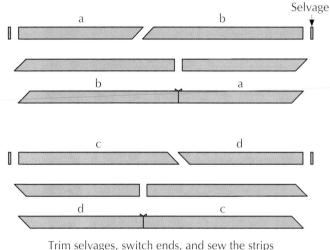

Trim selvages, switch ends, and sew the strips back together again.

Tip: Because it's difficult to keep the angled ends perfectly lined up while sewing the color runs, you may decide to trim all slant strips to the length of the shortest one before sewing them together.

---

4. Sew the cut strips together into color runs by chain piecing. To chain-piece, stitch a continuous seam without lifting the presser foot or cutting the threads between strips. Align the strips so that the edges of the color run will be smooth. As shown in "Making Straight Color Runs" on page 11, sew from left to right and then from right to left to avoid bowed color runs.

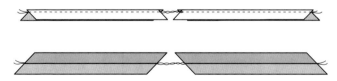

5. After you have completed stitching all strips of one fabric, clip the threads between the units. Press the seam allowances toward the lightest fabric. Continue adding strips to complete the color run.

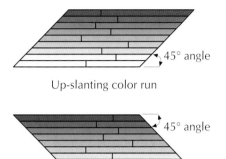

Up-slanting color run

Down-slanting color run

Making Slant Tubes

1. To trim the ends of each color run on a 45° angle, carefully align the lower edge of the color run with one of the cutting mat's horizontal lines and trim as far as possible, shifting the color run, if necessary, to complete the cut.

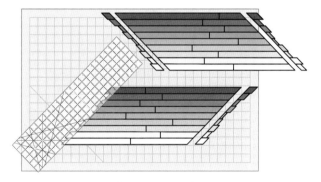

Trim ends on a 45° angle.

2. Sew one or more color runs into a tube, joining the lightest and the darkest strips. (Your project's size and design will determine how many color runs you need for each tube.) Press the seam allowances toward the darkest strip.

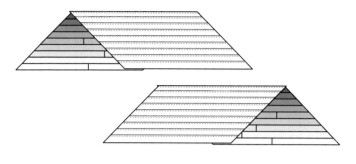

Stitch final seam to create tube.

3. Trim the uneven cut edge by carefully lining up the folds with the lines on the cutting mat and cutting perpendicular to the folds.

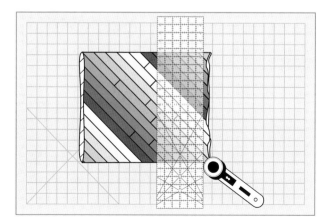

4. Referring to the Cutting Chart in the pattern directions, cut loops from the tube using your standard quilter's ruler. If making an original quilt, refer to your graphed design for the width of the loops; remember to add ½" for seam allowances.

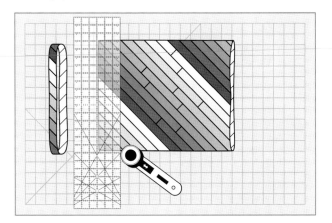

In some patterns, the color runs are not sewn into tubes, but rather are cut into Bargello strips. When cutting these strips from the color runs, be sure to line up the straight edge of the color run with the vertical lines on the cutting mat and the 45° seams with the diagonal line. Trim the edge of the color run as needed to keep the angles correct.

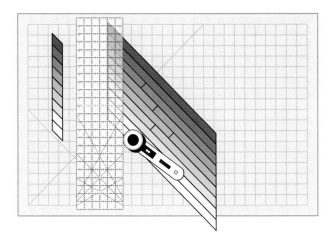

Pattern Direction

How you cut your color-run strips—crosswise or on the diagonal—affects the direction of the fabric's pattern. When you cut strips crosswise, from selvage to selvage, directional prints will look as though they bend with the design angles.

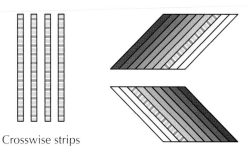

Crosswise strips

Cutting color-run strips on the diagonal requires more fabric, but the strips will be longer. Directional prints may go horizontally in some places and vertically in others.

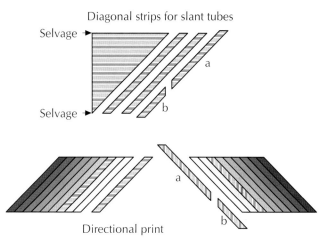

Diagonal strips for slant tubes

Selvage ➤

Selvage ➤

a

b

Directional print

a

b

You may want strips that always go in the same direction. In that case, cut three different types of strips for the color runs and tubes.

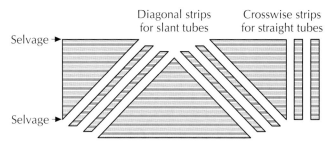

Diagonal strips for slant tubes

Crosswise strips for straight tubes

Selvage ➤

Selvage ➤

Creating the Curve

With regular Bargello, the Bargello strips are straight, and they move up or down in a predetermined way to create the curve. In matched-seam construction, the fabric rectangles in the Bargello strips move up or down one whole block height. With staggered seams, they move up or down one-half a block height. Drama in the curve depends upon the width of the color-run strips and the width of the Bargello strips.

With slant Bargello, each Bargello strip already slopes up or down at a 45° angle, creating a built-in curve. This angle actually prevents the quilter from achieving a lot of variation in the curve of the design, so visual excitement depends on other tricks. Reversing the order of the strips, so that they slope in the opposite direction of the curve, is one trick. This technique allows the quiltmaker to control the steepness of the curve design.

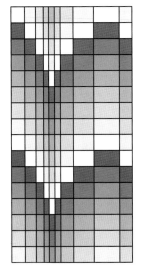

Matched-seam construction

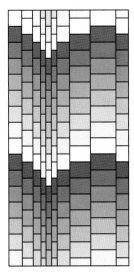

Staggered-seam construction

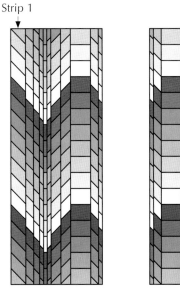
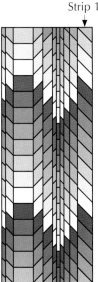

Strip 1

Strip 1

Regular slant Bargello

Reversed slant Bargello

Another technique is to disregard whether the seams are matched or staggered and arrange the strips in whatever style you wish. The quilt projects in this book make use of both of these tricks. Other slant Bargello projects ignore a graph and take advantage of geometric possibilities using strips from the color runs (see "St. Elmo's Fire" on page 75 and "Covenant" on page 68).

However, you may still need to make a graph to establish the curve and determine the quilt width, the number of Bargello strips you'll need, and the cut width of the Bargello strips.

Making a Paper Graph

Designing a curve on graph paper takes practice, but knowing how will help you plan and complete your own Bargello projects.

1. Photocopy the graph on page 7. Each small, narrow rectangle on this graph paper represents ¼" on your quilt. Disregard the vertical dimensions of each square. They correspond to the width of the color-run strips, which varies from project to project.

2. On the graph paper, indicate the width of the Bargello project you have in mind (not including the borders) and sketch a curved line across the design area.

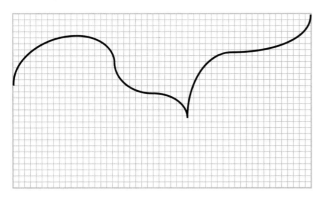

3. Determine the width of each block required to imitate your curve. Using a pencil, fill in the blocks. These blocks represent the widths of the various Bargello strips needed for your design.

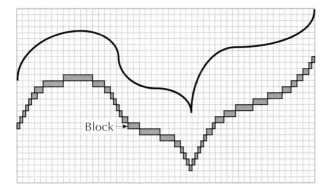

Block

Plan the block widths so the curve moves gracefully. Make use of repetitions in block width to achieve the slopes and design width that you drew.

An awkward but dynamic curve. There is no plan for determining block width as the curve changes.

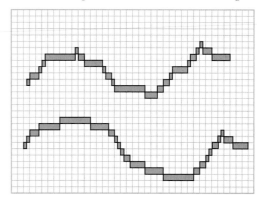

A graceful, calm curve. Notice that the blocks gradually widen or decrease in width, and some block sizes are repeated.

Remember that each narrow rectangle on the graph represents ¼" of the finished Bargello strip. Add ½" to each block for seam allowances when you cut a loop off your tube or a Bargello strip off your color run.

To optimize the color runs you constructed, don't use more blocks for your quilt than you have inches of width in the design. In other words, if you have 33" of Bargello design indicated on your graph, incorporate no more than 33 strips and, therefore, 33 blocks in your curve.

Use a variety of wide and narrow Bargello strips for a dynamic effect, but don't use too many narrow strips or your quilt will be dense and heavy. Strips wider than 3" can be secured by quilting when you finish your project.

Preparing the Backing and Batting

For this sew-and-flip technique, I prefer a thin, white polyester fleece that comes on a bolt at about 45" wide.

I recommend that you do *not* use cotton batting. For "Year of the Dragon" (page 55), I purchased a high-quality, very low-loft, queen-sized cotton batting because I wanted to avoid joining large pieces of fleece. But the cotton batting left avalanches of dust bunnies all over the house, and it had a tendency to "walk," no matter how well I pinned the layers. This shifting also created a bias pull, and I found it difficult to keep the horizon on the horizontal line. It did, however, result in a very soft and cozy bed cover, much more pliable than quilts made with polyester fleece.

Also avoid high-loft batting; it creates a tube effect down the quilt and catches in the tips of many presser feet.

You may prefer to use flannel instead of a traditional batting. These projects have considerable weight because of the seam allowances, so the flannel may be just right for your needs. Fleece gives the most body and is therefore excellent for wall quilts, but flannel is lighter and probably better for bed quilts.

The following instructions are for a typical Bargello project. Some of the patterns in this book specify a different preparation because of the construction techniques.

1. Wash and iron the backing fabric and construct the backing to your size requirements. Make the backing about 2" larger on all sides than the finished size of your project, including borders and binding. If you are using flannel for your batting, wash and iron it and piece it as necessary to match the backing. If you must piece batting, overlap and zigzag the raw edges to make the seam inconspicuous.

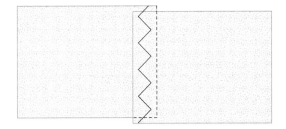

2. Place the backing wrong side up and lay the batting on top. Working from the center to the sides, smooth out the wrinkles. If you use a striped or gridded flannel, place it right side down on the backing so the lines show through as little as possible.

3. Secure the two layers with safety pins placed in a grid pattern every 8" across the surface. Remove the pins as you attach the Bargello strips.

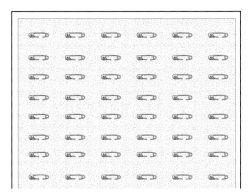

4. With a No. 2 pencil, draw a vertical line down the center of the batting from top to bottom. Make sure the line is straight and perpendicular to the top and bottom edges, since it is the guide for the first Bargello strip. You will align subsequent Bargello strips according to the first strip.

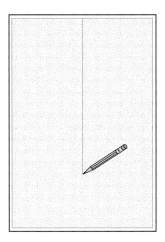

5. If you are not using striped or gridded flannel for your batting, use a wide quilter's ruler to mark parallel lines from the center line to the edges of the batting. Space the lines approximately 6" apart. For a complex piece or a miniature, space the lines 3" apart. Refer to these lines when placing the Bargello strips as you work from the center to the outer edges of the quilt (see "Troubleshooting" on page 29).

6. Mark a horizontal line at the center, from side to side. Refer to this line to match the centers of the Bargello strips as you add them.

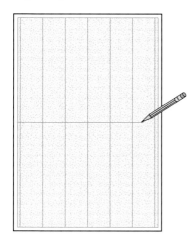

Cutting Tubes into Loops

Now you're set to cut your tubes into loops. As a reminder, loops cut from a straight tube have no slant. Loops cut from an up-slanting tube point up and those cut from a down-slanting tube point down.

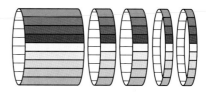

Loops cut from straight tube

Loops cut from   Loops cut from
up-slanting tube   down-slanting tube

1. Trim the raw edges of the tube and carefully check the layers to make sure that the edges are even, with no rough spots.

2. Cut loops from your three types of tubes using a standard quilter's ruler, checking to see whether the loops will be used for straight, up-slanting, or down-slanting Bargello strips. Refer to the Cutting Chart in each pattern or your graph, if your design is original, for the cut widths of the loops. If working from your graph, remember to add ½" to the finished width of each Bargello strip. As you cut each loop, make sure you have cut through all thicknesses before lifting your ruler.

Tip: If you must take a break from cutting loops, insert about four pins near the cut ends of your tubes, securing the edges so they remain straight and aligned.

Arranging Loops
on Your Design Wall

In many of the projects in this book, you have design choices to make about how to arrange the loops for the most attractive curve. As you cut loops off the tubes, pin them onto your design wall in order. Once you have cut and pinned all the loops, try rotating them to see how they work best together. Re-pin each rotated loop onto your design wall.

Loops as they are cut from the three tubes

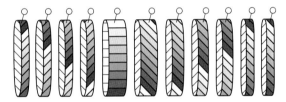

Loops after they are rotated for an attractive curve

Opening Loops to
Make Bargello Strips

After you have established the curve, you are ready to turn your loops into Bargello strips. On straight loops, you can cut across the loop or remove stitches from one of the seams using a seam ripper. Strips made by removing the stitches will be ½" longer than those that result from cutting the loops.

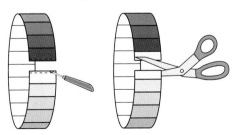

To make a loop from an up- or down-slanting tube into a Bargello strip, cut across the loop. Remember that the loops cannot easily be re-created: cut them only when you're sure you're cutting in the right place. If you make a mistake, cut a new loop from your tube or repair the loop with leftover color-run fabric.

One at a time, open each loop into a strip, allowing the back half of the strip to fall down to its full length. Pin each strip to your design wall.

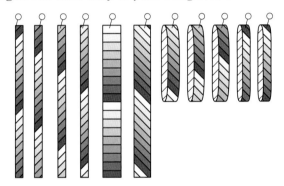

As you prepare your Bargello strips, remember that loops cut from slant tubes will stretch if handled too much or too roughly. Don't let them hang overnight on your design wall, or they will be much longer than their straight-of-grain partners by morning.

NOTE: *In some patterns, the color runs are not sewn into tubes. Rather, you cut them into segments, which you then join to make Bargello strips.*

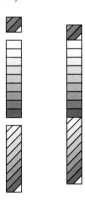

Stitching Bargello Strips

1. Refer to your pattern or graph to determine which Bargello strip is in the center of your quilt. Fold the strip to find its center and place this fold on the horizontal line. Gently stretch the strip, right side up, along the vertical center line.

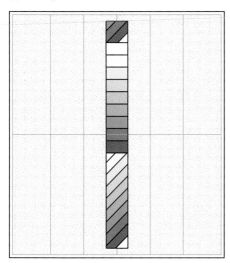

The first strip may not be centered on the vertical line, depending on its location on the graphed curve, so refer to your pattern for proper placement.

2. Pin the Bargello strip securely through all layers in each fabric segment.

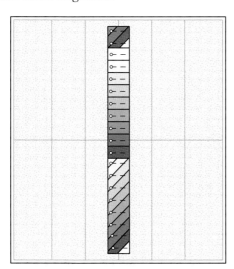

3. Unpin the Bargello strip to the right of the center strip on your design wall. Match the center of the strip to the horizontal pencil line. Match any seams that are important to your design.

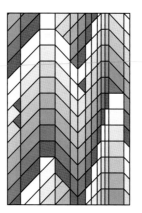 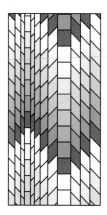

Pattern where seams should match well   Pattern where seams don't need to match

NOTE: *When you add the strips, straight strips with pulled-out seams will extend up or down ¼" farther than strips created by cutting loops.*

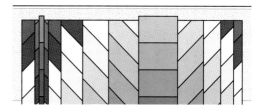

4. Gently stretch the strip, being careful of the bias. Lay the second strip on the first, right sides facing and raw edges aligned. Pin the strips together at every seam, placing the pins toward the sewing machine and ¼" from the edges of the strips, along the future seam. Placing the pins toward the sewing machine makes it easy to remove each pin as the top strip feeds into the machine. It also enables you to carefully check the strips while they are still pinned to ensure that your seam line will be smooth and accurate.

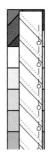 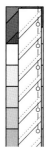

5. Machine stitch the Bargello strips through all layers, being careful to keep the seam straight. Remove each pin as it reaches the presser foot; pulling a pin out too early can distort the Bargello strip. Use a seam ripper to carefully remove only the crooked part of any "glitch" that may occur.

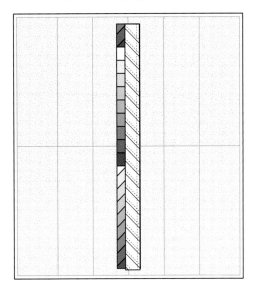

Depending on the direction of the pressed seam allowances, you may be forced to stitch against the seam allowances on some strips. Don't be concerned; pin carefully and stitch slowly.

To keep the back neat, pull the bobbin thread to the front at the start and finish of each seam, and whenever you rip and re-sew part of a seam. Knot the top and bobbin threads if you wish and let the ends hang; they will be covered up by Bargello strips, borders, and binding.

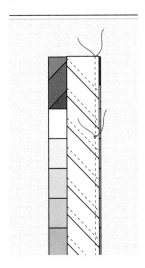

6. Flip the strip to the right and press it out with your palm or iron. Pin the free edge of the strip smoothly and tightly, placing the pins on the diagonal for easy removal.

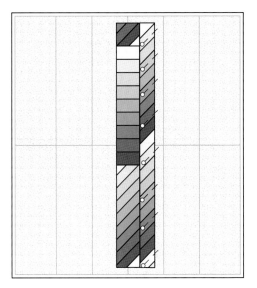

Be careful not to pull out the stitching in the segments of the Bargello strip before adding the next strip. If a little of this occurs, don't worry: stitching the next Bargello strip to the backing and batting will secure the edges.

7. Position and pin the next strip to the right in the design sequence. Remove the diagonal pins. Stitch; flip the strip, press, and pin.

8. Continue to add Bargello strips until you reach the right edge of the quilt; return to the center and add strips until you reach the left edge. Now you're nearly finished! Each strip will be an exciting addition to your beautiful design.

Tip: Narrow Bargello strips that are ¼" wide when finished are nice to include in a design for dramatic, steep slopes and bold points. I like to place three or four of these strips together in a few parts of my curve. Stitching narrow strips to a uniform width is difficult if you sew them in the usual manner. Inserting the pins in the opposite direction makes sewing narrow strips easier. Here's how:

1. Turn the quilt around, with the top of the quilt at the bottom. Pin the next strip to the quilt, with the pins pointing up, toward what was the bottom of the quilt.

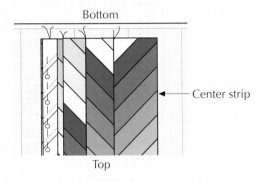

Bottom

Center strip

Top

2. Put the bobbin thread on top; put the top thread in the bobbin. Flip the quilt over and stitch from the backing side, using the previous stitching as a guide. Reach under the quilt and pull out the pins from the front as you stitch, making sure the seam allowances are flat.

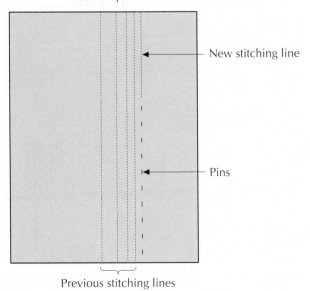

Back of quilt

New stitching line

Pins

Previous stitching lines

BORDERS AND BINDING

Several of the quilts in this book have so much excitement in the Bargello design that a complex finishing would detract from the impact of the pieces. Others are quite successful with several different borders and a wide binding. When your project is finished, place folded leftover fabrics against the edges to see what works best. Then use a ruler to determine the measurements. To the finished width of each border, add ½" for seam allowances.

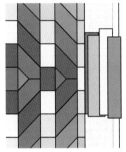 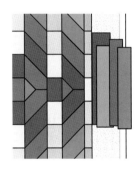

First attempt   Final decision

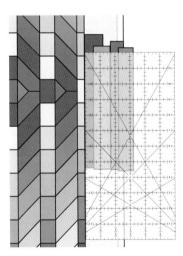

Border 1: ⅝" finished, 1⅛" strips
Border 2: ⅞" finished, 1⅜" strips
Border 3: ½" finished, 1" strips
Binding: 1" finished, 1½" strips

Adding Borders

Attach borders the same way that you sew Bargello strips to the quilt: stitch one strip at a time, flip it over, and hand-press if desired. Adding the borders in this manner creates a nice firm edge on the quilt. Stitch the side borders first, then the top and bottom borders.

1. Starting from the center horizontal line, measure up and down to determine the maximum height of the design area, which is the distance to the ends of the shortest Bargello strips. Place pins at that distance from the horizontal line along the top and bottom. Some strips will undoubtedly stick up or down farther than others.

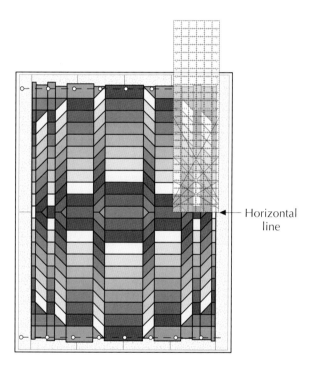

← Horizontal line

2. Measure through the center of the quilt from pin line to pin line to determine how long to cut your side borders. Piece strips, if necessary. Cut the border strips to the correct length.

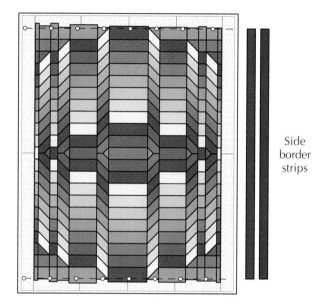

Side border strips

3. Mark or place a pin at the center and quarter points along the sides of the quilt, from pin line to pin line. Repeat with the border strips.

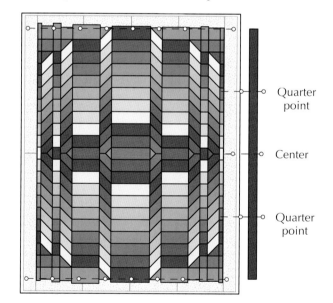

Quarter point

Center

Quarter point

4. Lay the side border strips, right sides down, on the outer Bargello strips, positioning the border strips to hide small imperfections in the Bargello strips. Pin each border to the quilt top along the edges, matching ends and marked points and easing fullness, if necessary. Stitch the borders, using the edges of the border strips as your guide. Flip the borders out, hand-press, and pin.

Seam line for
side border strip
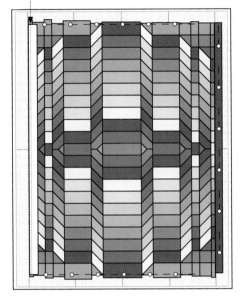

5. For the top and bottom borders, measure across the center of the quilt from raw edge to raw edge, including the side borders. Piece strips, if necessary. Cut the border strips to the correct measurement.

Top and bottom border strips
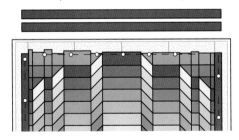

6. Align the raw edges of the top and bottom border strips with the pin lines across the Bargello strips; pin. Stitch, flip, hand-press, and pin the borders as you did the side borders.

Seam line for top
border strip
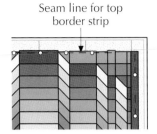

7. Repeat steps 2–6 for the remaining borders.

Binding Your Quilt

Some quilters use binding strips cut on the bias. I never do, yet I am satisfied with the way my bindings lie, flat and smooth.

I prefer single-thickness binding because it is less bulky than double-fold binding. Be sure to miter your corners with nice sharp points. With the precision built into Bargello design, you must also try for precise finishing.

1. Decide how wide you want the finished binding to be. Subtract ¼" from the finished binding width to determine where to trim the backing and batting in relation to the outer border. For example, if you want a 1" bound edge, trim the backing and batting so ¾" extends beyond the outer border. The distance from the stitching line to the edge will be 1".

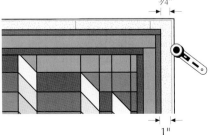

3/4"

1"

If you prefer a more traditional ¼"-wide binding, trim the backing and batting even with the raw edges of the outer border.

2. For single-thickness binding, cut the strips two times the finished width, plus ½" for seams. For instance, for a bound edge that will be 1" wide, cut the binding strips 2½" wide. Cut enough strips to go all the way around, plus 6 strip widths' extra length for overlapped seams and corners.

3. Piece your binding strips at a 45° angle to reduce bulk.

4. Place the binding strip along the raw edges of the border as shown. Leaving 3" free at the beginning of the binding, stitch, using a ¼"-wide seam allowance. Stop stitching ¼" from the edge of the outer border strip.

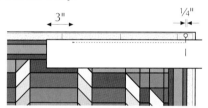

5. Fold the binding away from the quilt, creating a 45° angle as shown.

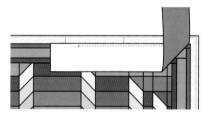

6. Fold the binding back at the *upper edge of the quilt* and align the binding's raw edges with the edges of the outer border strip. Starting at the upper edge of the quilt, stitch, using a ¼"-wide seam allowance.

Upper edge of quilt

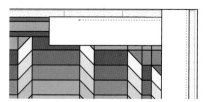

7. Stitch the binding to all four sides and miter the corners as directed in steps 5 and 6. Lap the end of the binding over the beginning. The overlap should equal two times the cut width of the binding. Cut the overlapped end on a 45° angle as shown.

Beginning   End

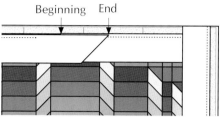

8. Trim the beginning of the binding to overlap the angled end ½". With right sides together, stitch the ends, using a ¼"-wide seam allowance. Complete the binding stitching.

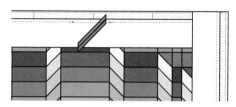

9. Turn the binding to the back and fold under ¼" on the raw edge. Sew the fold to the stitching on the back using a blind stitch.

10. Miter the corners on both sides as you stitch the binding to the back. If desired, stitch along the miter fold.

Fold second.

Fold first.

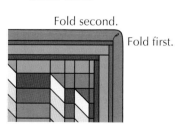 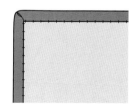

Front of quilt   Back of quilt

TROUBLESHOOTING

As with any endeavor, preventing problems is much more efficient than correcting them. There are ways to prevent common problems that occur in slant Bargello:

◆ Use a sewing machine in good working order.
◆ Choose fabrics of a uniform and high quality. Although I seldom follow my own advice, I do have fewer difficulties when all the fabrics in my color run are of a similar type and quality.
◆ Cut and sew your color-run strips carefully and consistently. If one strip is wider than the others or doesn't have straight edges, your color runs and tubes will not have the correct 45° slant.
◆ Make sure your 45° angle is accurate. When the slope is greater or less than it should be, the strips will not meet properly if you are matching the seams.
◆ Do not use cotton batting! See "Preparing the Backing and Batting" on page 20.
◆ I do not iron my strips after I sew each one down. Flipping them out and smoothing them with the palm of my hand has always worked well for me. However, if you have a problem with bias stretch, you may want to press your strips as you go.
◆ If you continue having problems with the bias and your strips stretch as you sew them down, try easing the presser-foot tension on your sewing machine. A walking foot or a machine with even feed will prevent these problems. Or use a small screwdriver or a long pin to "walk" your fabric backward as you sew the seam.
◆ Some quilts require matching seams. If your seams do not match, focus on matching the seams where the contrast in your color runs is the greatest.

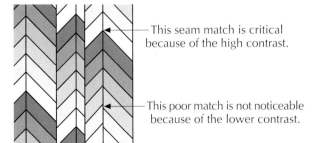

This seam match is critical because of the high contrast.

This poor match is not noticeable because of the lower contrast.

◆ As you sew the Bargello strips, especially when matching the seams, the top and bottom edges of your Bargello design may become crooked. Don't be concerned; the top and bottom borders will cover any uneven edges. If your finished design is an inch or so shorter than the dimension specified in the pattern, and a little of the design is cut off by the borders, it doesn't matter. My quilts are the same way!
◆ However, if your left and right edges begin to waver, take steps to correct the problem. Make small alterations in pinning and sewing subsequent strips to straighten the sides.

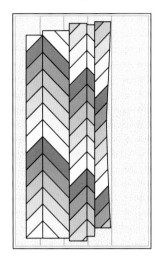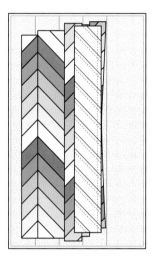

◆ Compare your quilt with the graph measurements as you go. For example, after you complete 9¼" of graphed design, your piece should measure 9¾" wide, which includes ¼" for the seam allowance on each edge. If the quilt is turning out narrower than it should, take slightly narrower seams in subsequent strips. If the quilt is too wide, take slightly wider seams until the project is the correct width.
◆ Be sure to place your strips properly on the horizontal line. Otherwise, your quilt will become a parallelogram.

As precise as these quilts look, a certain amount of fudging is involved. Don't be afraid to put that old standby trick to use when needed.

CONNECTING UPWARD AND DOWNWARD CURVES

In regular Bargello, accent strips sewn between the main Bargello strips act as separator strips. In slant Bargello designs, you may want to incorporate "connecting" Bargello strips made from slant-Bargello color runs or tubes. These can help create exciting "architectural" structures.

Separator strips

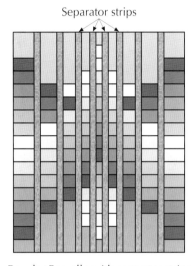

Regular Bargello with separator strips

Connector strips

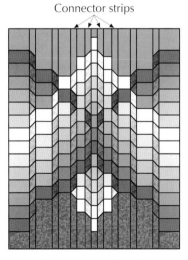

Combination Bargello with slant connector strips

The width of these connecting Bargello strips must be related to the width of the strips used in the straight color runs and tubes. The finished width of the connecting strips may be the same as the finished width of the straight color-run strips, one-half the width, twice that width, and so on. This relationship enables the design to form a pathway through your quilt.

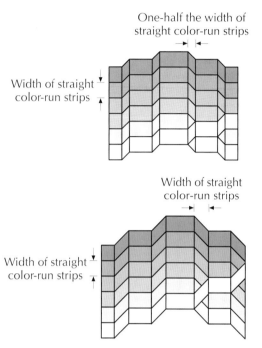

If you want to include narrower connecting strips, you should have narrower strips in your straight color runs. To maintain the desired finished width of the color run, you'll need to use more color-run strips.

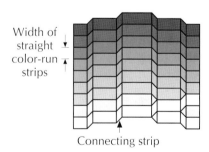

These additional design strips allow you to create the illusion of dimension and depth to your piece (see "Crystal City" on page 81).

USING COLOR CHANGES TO CREATE DIMENSION

You can create even more architectural structure in your quilts by making your straight and slant color runs from different fabrics. One easy approach is to make the slant color runs with slightly different fabrics from those in the straight color runs. They may be darker overall, or duller. Or, you might choose solids for the straight color runs and prints for the slant color runs. This subtle difference can suggest that the slant part of your design is a side view of a building or folded structure. Notice the difference in these two simple designs.

You can also achieve the illusion of a reflection in water by varying the fabrics in portions of the quilt. For "Rainy Day at Pine Creek" (page 90), I chose richer colors for the fabrics used in the upper half of the design and duller versions for those in the lower half. This variation creates the impression of a slightly muddy river with trees at its edge. I made two sets of each type of tube: a straight, up-slanting, and down-slanting tube in the brighter fabrics and each tube in the duller tones. I also used a few scraps of the richer colors in the lower half of the design to suggest reflections.

Reflection across a horizon with some fabric
substitutions in the lower portion

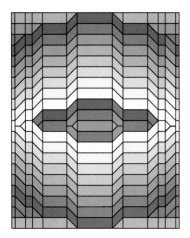

Design using one set of fabrics
for the color runs

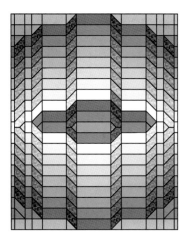

Design using one set of fabrics for the
straight color runs and another for the
slant color runs

FLOATING A DESIGN ON A PLAIN BACKGROUND

A slant Bargello design can have a powerful visual impact when background areas are left solid. Compare the drawing below with "St. Elmo's Fire" on page 75. In the drawing, I tried to completely fill in the composition with Bargello strips and square it up by trimming some portions, but I finally realized that it was best left more open. In the quilt, I used a black print that reads as a near-solid fabric for the background.

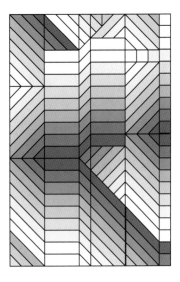

You might also decide to substitute background fabric for some of your Bargello strips. The contrast can be very exciting.

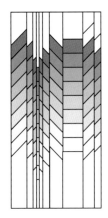

Float the slant Bargello design strips on a plain background for a dramatic effect.

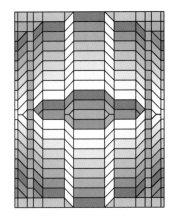

Use solid or pieced sections of background fabrics for Bargello strips, slant or straight, to individualize your piece.

PATTERNS

For the projects in this section, you'll find directions for strips that are cut straight, from selvage to selvage. If you wish to cut your strips on the diagonal for the slant color runs, you'll need more fabric. (See "Pattern Direction" on page 17.) All patterns use 100% cotton fabric that is at least 42" wide. Seam allowances are ¼" wide.

When a pattern includes a template, the straight of grain is vertical on the template, unless otherwise noted. Be sure to consider carefully the way you cut directional prints. If you plan to cut your color-run strips on the diagonal, you may want to change the straight-of-grain line on the template so the pattern runs in the same direction throughout the quilt.

For "Vail," "Covenant," "St. Elmo's Fire," and "Crystal City," you will need to cut pieces using small diagrams rather than full-size templates. Use standard graph paper and follow the measurements on the diagrams carefully to draw and cut accurate shapes.

I've included approximately 4" extra in backing and batting measurements to allow a 2" buffer zone on all sides during construction. My friend Lori Kuba, who made two of the quilts in the gallery, increased her backing and batting sizes because she wanted wider borders than called for in the pattern. Plan for that, if desired, before cutting your fabric and batting.

By Marge Edie, 1996, Clemson, South Carolina. In my imagination, this is what a New England autumn looks like. Fall colors and naturalistic prints create a peaceful hillside setting.

*A*lthough "Vermont" has a lot of vitality, it is technically very simple to make and is, therefore, a great project for starters. You'll find a graph, with an indication of the steepness of the slopes, but you may pick your own strip arrangement and incline for the up-and-down slant. Colors to match autumn trees, underwater grottoes, or stalactite-filled caves are all appropriate and attractive.

Materials: 42"-wide fabric

¼ yd. *each* of 10 fabrics for Bargello strips

1⅜ yds. for backing

32" x 47" rectangle of batting

¼ yd. for inner border

¼ yd. for outer border

¼ yd. for binding

Directions

Read the Bargello instructions on pages 10–28 before you begin and refer to them for each step in the quiltmaking process.

1. Cut 1 strip, 2½" wide, from each of the 10 fabrics for the Bargello strips. Construct 1 straight color run. The strips will measure 2" wide when finished, and the color run will measure 20½" wide. Press the seams toward the light fabrics.

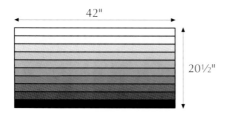

42"

20½"

Straight color run

2. Cut the color run in half and stitch the sections together to make 1 half-width tube.

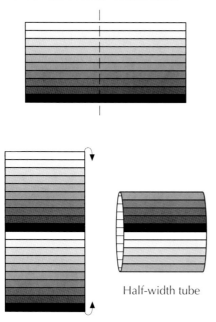

Half-width tube

3. Cut 3 strips from each of the 10 fabrics using the Bias Stripper ruler at the 2" mark; each strip will measure approximately 1⅞" wide.

4. Using 10 strips, construct 1 up-slanting color run. The strips will measure approximately 1⅜" wide when finished. The color run will measure approximately 14⅝" across, from the lightest to the darkest strip, and 20½" on the diagonal edge. Trim the ends of the color run.

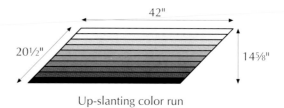

42"

20½"

14⅝"

Up-slanting color run

5. Cut the color run in half on the 45° diagonal to create 2 half-width color runs. Stitch the sections together to make 1 half-width tube.

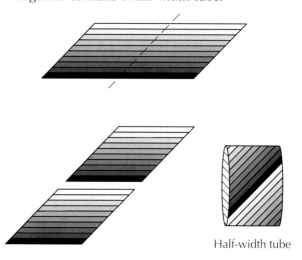

Half-width tube

6. Using the remaining strips, construct 2 down-slanting color runs.

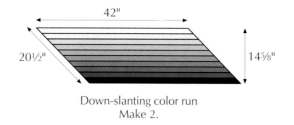

42"

20½"

14⅝"

Down-slanting color run
Make 2.

Stitch the 2 color runs together into a tube.

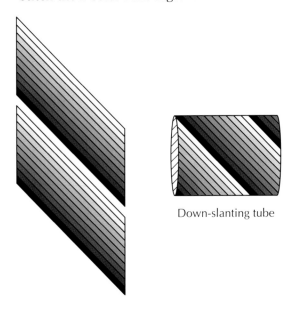

Down-slanting tube

When the tubes are folded flat, they should measure 20" from fold to fold.

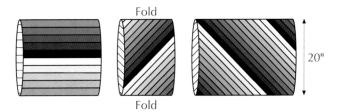

Fold

Fold

20"

7. Refer to the graph below and the Cutting Chart on the next page for the placement and cut width of the Bargello strips. Notice that as the curve moves up, you cut the loops from the down-slanting tube. As the curve moves down, you cut them from the up-slanting tube. When the curve changes direction, the loops are cut from the straight tube.

Cut the loops from the tubes using your standard quilter's ruler.

Grid squares equal ¼".
Measurements are for *finished* strip widths.

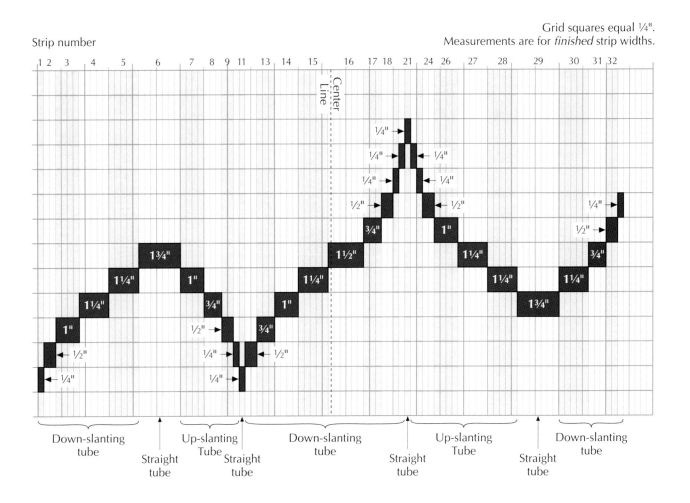

Cut from Straight Tube

Strip No.	No. of Strips per Set	Cut Strip Width	Finished Strip Width
11, 21	2	3/4"	1/4"
6, 28	2	2 1/4"	1 3/4"

Cut from Up-Slanting Tube

Strip No.	No. of Strips per Set	Cut Strip Width	Finished Strip Width
10, 22, 23	3	3/4"	1/4"
9, 24	2	1"	1/2"
8	1	1 1/4"	3/4"
7, 25	2	1 1/2"	1"
26, 27	2	1 3/4"	1 1/4"

Cut from Down-Slanting Tube

Strip No.	No. of Strips per Set	Cut Strip Width	Finished Strip Width
1, 19, 20, 32	4	3/4"	1/4"
2, 12, 18, 31	4	1"	1/2"
13, 17, 30	3	1 1/4"	3/4"
3, 14	2	1 1/2"	1"
4, 5, 15, 29	4	1 3/4"	1 1/4"
16	1	2"	1 1/2"

8. Rotate the loops to achieve the desired steepness in the slope, or refer to the quilt plan on page 34 and the illustration below for help in creating the curves. Once you establish the curves, open the loops at the top and let the Bargello strips hang down your design wall.

Strip number

1 2 3 4 5 6 7 8 9 10 11 12 13 14 15 16 17 18 19 20 21 22 23 24 25 26 27 28 29 30 31 32

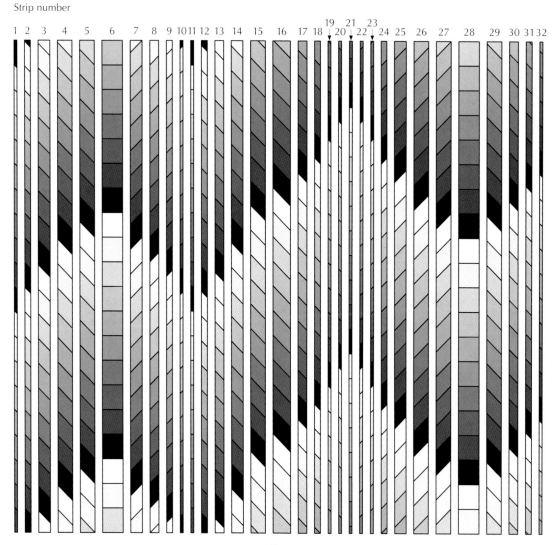

Bargello strips

9. If desired, create tree trunks and branches in your Bargello design, as in the photo on page 33. Following the diagram below, separate the seams in your Bargello strips where you wish to insert the branches and trunks (A).

To make a slanting tree branch, trim ¼" from a fabric segment (B). To make a trunk, trim ¼" from one long edge of a section of Bargello strip (C).

Replace the trimmed areas with ¾"-wide strips of fabric, first for the trunks (D), then for the branches (E). Re-sew the seams. The branches and trunks will finish to ¼" wide (F).

10. Prepare the backing and batting.
11. Place Strip 16 on the center line and place Strip 17 on top, right sides together; pin. Stitch, using a ¼"-wide seam allowance, along the right edges of the strips. Flip Strip 17 to the right and press as necessary.

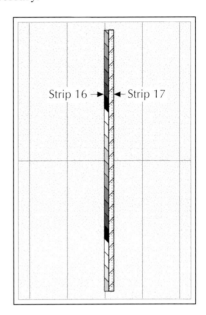

Strip 16 → ← Strip 17

5   6   7   8   13   14   16   26   28

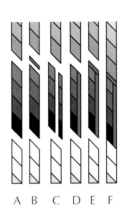

A B C D E F

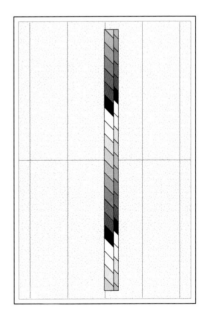

12. Continue sewing the Bargello strips to the quilt, working from the center to the right edge.
13. Return to the center and add the Bargello strips to the left, starting with Strip 15 and working toward the left edge.

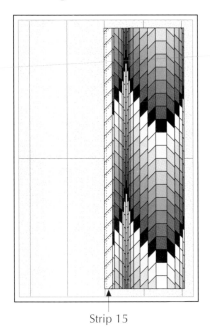

Strip 15

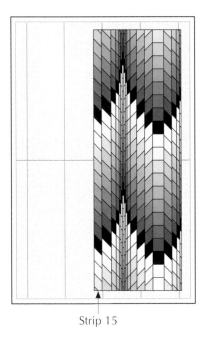

Strip 15

Borders and Binding

1. From the inner border fabric, cut 4 strips, each ⅞" wide. Join the strips as needed. Sew the side inner borders to the quilt top; then add the top and bottom inner borders. The border will measure ⅜" wide when finished.
2. From the outer border fabric, cut 4 strips, each 1¼" wide. Join the strips as needed. If desired, add a 1¼" square of the darkest fabric to the lower border strip to extend the lower Bargello curve point.

1¼" square

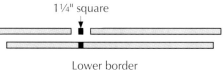

Lower border

Sew the borders to the quilt, following the directions in step 1. The border will measure ¾" wide when finished.

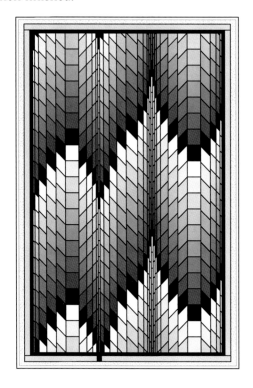

3. Trim the batting and backing, leaving ¼" extending beyond the edge of the outer border.
4. From the binding fabric, cut 4 strips, each 1½" wide, for single-thickness binding. Join the ends with a 45° diagonal seam. Bind the quilt. The binding will measure ½" wide when finished.

Tidal Pool

FINISHED SIZE: 25" x 32½"

By Marge Edie, 1997, Clemson, South Carolina. This simple geometry is a great project for beginning Bargello enthusiasts. The brilliant palette was presented to me as a challenge by my friend Dori Hawks, to push me beyond my fondness for peach and olive green. To explore the possibilities in a simple Bargello structure, I quickly made four variations (page 89) on the design. All five quilts were completed in about ten days.

Materials: 42"-wide fabric

¼ yd. *each* of 4 fabrics, from light to medium,
for Bargello strips

⅜ yd. *each* of 4 fabrics, from medium to dark,
for Bargello strips

⅞ yd. for backing

29" x 37" rectangle of batting

¼ yd. for binding

Directions

Read the Bargello instructions on pages 10–28 before you begin and refer to them for each step in the quiltmaking process.

1. Cut 1 strip, 2" wide, from each of the 8 fabrics for the Bargello strips. Construct 1 straight color run. The strips will measure 1½" wide when finished, and the color run will measure 12½" wide. Press the seams toward the light fabrics.

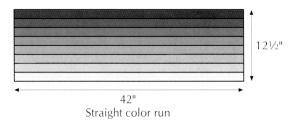

12½"

42"
Straight color run

2. Cut 1 strip from each of the 8 fabrics using the Bias Stripper ruler at the 1½" mark; each strip will measure slightly more than 1½" wide. Cut each strip in half.

3. Construct a half-width up-slanting color run and a half-width down-slanting color run. The strips will measure slightly more than 1" wide when finished. The color runs will measure approximately 8⅞" across, from the lightest to the darkest strip, and 12½" on the diagonal edge.

Half-width up-slanting color run

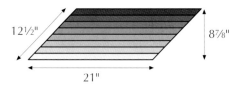

12½"

8⅞"

21"

Half-width down-slanting color run

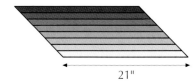

21"

"*T*idal Pool" is a good starter project because it incorporates all the skills required for slant Bargello, but on a small scale. The structure has many possible variations—check them out on page 89. These quilts are the most exciting of the twelve I designed on the computer before making the quilt you see here.

If desired, plan to incorporate separator strips for further interest, as in "Tidal Pool III." Subtract ¼" from the width of each straight Bargello strip and add a ¾"-wide strip of separator fabric, which will finish to ¼". Separator strips are especially useful for hiding unmatchable seam lines. Also notice the background variations in the gallery quilts; you may want to use a different arrangement of fill-in shapes in your piece.

4. Refer to the Cutting Chart below for the placement and cut width of the Bargello strips. Cut the strips from the 3 color runs using your standard quilter's ruler. Following the diagram below, arrange the Bargello strips on your design wall. Remove the lightest rectangle from the top of the lower color runs in Strips 1 and 13. Use the trimming template on page 45 to trim the point from the darkest fabric in the slant color runs in Strips 2 and 12.

Cut from Up-Slanting Color Run

Strip No.	No. of Strips per Set	Cut Strip Width	Finished Strip Width
2, 4, 6, 8, 10, 12	6	2"	1½"

Cut from Down-Slanting Color Run

Strip No.	No. of Strips per Set	Cut Strip Width	Finished Strip Width
2, 4, 6, 8, 10, 12	6	2"	1½"

Cut from Straight Color Run

Strip No.	No. of Strips per Set	Cut Strip Width	Finished Strip Width
1, 13	4	1"	½"
3, 11	4	1½"	1"
5, 9	4	4"	3½"
7	2	5½"	5"

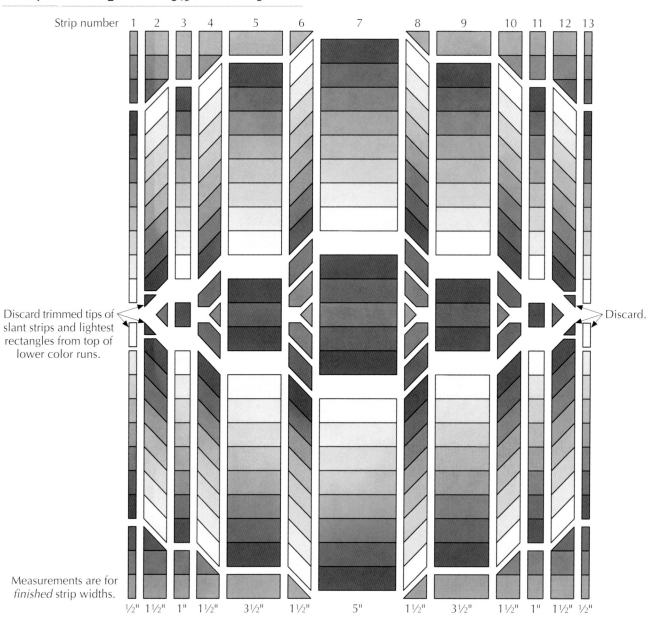

Strip number 1 2 3 4 5 6 7 8 9 10 11 12 13

Discard trimmed tips of slant strips and lightest rectangles from top of lower color runs.

Discard.

Measurements are for *finished* strip widths.

½" 1½" 1" 1½" 3½" 1½" 5" 1½" 3½" 1½" 1" 1½" ½"

5. Cut an extra strip, 2" wide, from each of fabrics 5, 6, 7, and 8. Referring to the Cutting Chart for the extra strips and the previous illustration, cut the pieces.

From Extra Strip of Color 5

Strip No.	No of Strips per Set	Cut Strip Width	Finished Strip Width
1, 13	4	1"	½"
2, 4, 10, 12	8	2"	1½"
3, 11	4	1½"	1"
5, 9	4	4"	3½"

From Extra Strip of Color 6

Strip No.	No. of Strips per Set	Cut Strip Width	Finished Strip Width
1, 13	4	1"	½"
2, 12	4	2"	1½"
3, 11	4	1½"	1"
7	1	5½"	5"

From Extra Strip of Color 7

Strip No.	No. of Strips per Set	Cut Strip Width	Finished Strip Width
1, 13	4	1"	½"
5, 9	2	4"	3½"
7	2	5½"	5"

From Extra Strip of Color 8

Strip No.	No of Strips per Set	Cut Strip Width	Finished Strip Width
3, 11	2	1½"	1"
5, 9	4	4"	3½"
7	2	5½"	5"

6. You'll also need triangles and odd-sized shapes to complete your Bargello strips. Trace the templates on page 45 and cut the following:

From *each* of fabrics 5, 6, and 7, cut:
    4 half-square triangles
    2 quarter-square triangles
Use these pieces in Strips 2, 4, 6, 8, 10, and 12.

From fabric 6, cut:
    2 and 2 reversed partial parallelograms
Use these pieces in Strips 6 and 8.

From fabric 7, cut:
    2 and 2 reversed parallelograms
    2 and 2 reversed partial parallelograms
Use these pieces in Strips 4, 6, 8, and 10.

7. Join the Bargello strips and pieces cut in steps 5 and 6 to make complete Bargello strips. See the piecing detail below for Strips 4, 6, 8, and 10.

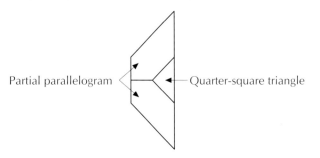

Partial parallelogram   Quarter-square triangle

8. Prepare the backing and batting.

9. Place Strip 7 on the center line and place Strip 8 on top, right sides together, matching the seams and triangle points as best you can. Pin. Stitch, using a ¼"-wide seam allowance, along the right edges of the strips. Flip Strip 8 to the right and press as necessary.

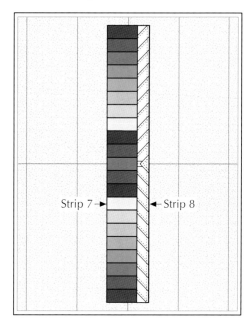

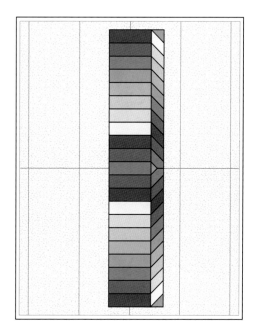

10. Continue adding Bargello strips to the right, working toward the right edge.

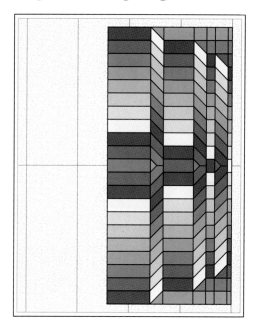

11. Return to the center and add the Bargello strips to the left, starting with Strip 7 and working toward the left edge.

Binding

1. Trim the backing and batting ¼" from the edges of the Bargello strips.
2. From the binding fabric, cut 4 strips, each 1½" wide, for single-thickness binding. Join the ends with a 45° diagonal seam. Bind the quilt. The binding will measure ½" wide when finished.

2¾" square

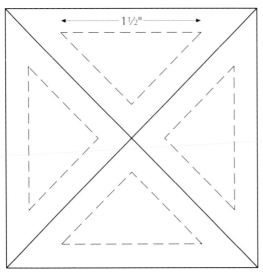

Quarter-square triangles
Cut 2 *each* from fabrics 5, 6, and 7.

2⅜" square

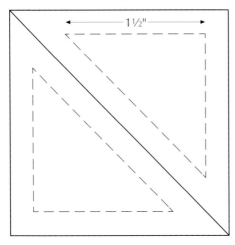

Half-square triangles
Cut 4 *each* from fabrics 5, 6, and 7.

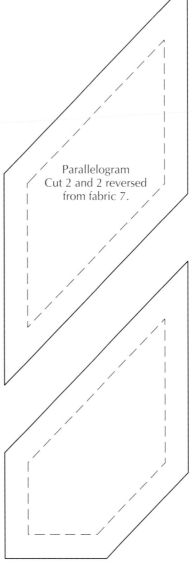

Parallelogram
Cut 2 and 2 reversed
from fabric 7.

Partial parallelogram
Cut 2 and 2 reversed from fabrics 6 and 7.
Trimming template for fabric 8.

Radiance

FINISHED SIZE: 45½" x 31¼"

By Marge Edie, 1997, Clemson, South Carolina. The special glow of Christmas—the candles, decorated trees, hearth fires, and family—is portrayed with brilliant hues and contrasting values in this holiday piece.

*T*his design is similar to "Rainy Day at Pine Lake" (page 90), except that the center horizon strips in "Pine Lake" finish to ½", and the fabrics for the bottom sections are duller, slightly lighter versions of the fabrics in the top of the quilt. Notice also that "Pine Lake" has strip enhancements to further the illusion that the trees are reflected in a pond or creek.

"Radiance" is a quick piece to make. I washed the fabrics and made the tubes last Friday, sewed the right-hand Bargello strips down on Saturday afternoon, the rest of the strips on Sunday afternoon, and the borders and binding on Monday. Now it's Wednesday afternoon, and I spent the morning hand stitching the binding to the back. It will take me three times as long to explain how to put this quilt together than it took to make it!

Materials: 42"-wide fabric

⅜ yd. *each* of 9 fabrics for
Bargello and horizon strips
1½ yds. for backing
50" x 34" rectangle of batting
¼ yd. *each* of 3 fabrics for borders
¼ yd. for binding

Directions

Read the Bargello instructions on pages 10–28 before you begin and refer to them for each step in the quiltmaking process.

1. Cut 1 strip, 2" wide, from each of the 9 fabrics for the Bargello strips. Construct 1 straight color run. The strips will measure 1½" wide when finished, and the color run will measure 14" wide. Press the seams toward the light fabrics. Sew the color run into a tube.

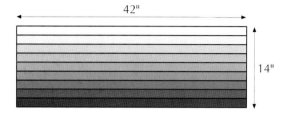

Straight tube

2. Cut 4 strips from each of the 9 fabrics using the Bias Stripper ruler at the 1½" mark; each strip will measure slightly more than 1½" wide. Sew 2 strips of each fabric together end to end to make a strip approximately 83½" long. Make 2 long strips of each fabric.

3. Construct 1 up-slanting color run and 1 down-slanting color run, each approximately 83½" long. The strips will measure slightly more than 1" wide when finished. The color runs will measure approximately 10" across, from the lightest to the darkest strip, and 14" on the diagonal edge.

4. Pin and then sew the long color runs into 1 up-slanting tube and 1 down-slanting tube. This step is awkward, but you'll find it easier if you twist each color run into a loose spiral before putting in the pins. The tubes will measure approximately 60" long.

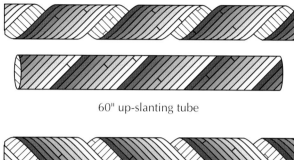

60" up-slanting tube

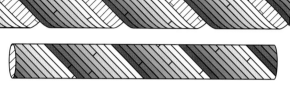

60" down-slanting tube

When the 3 tubes are folded flat, they will measure 6¾" from fold to fold.

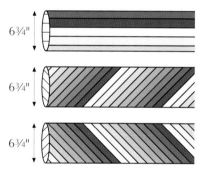

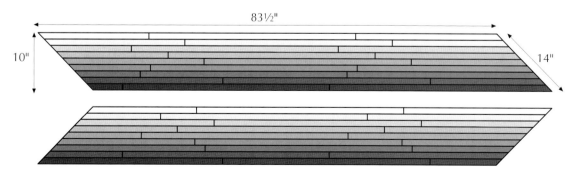

Assembling the Quilt

This quilt consists of three major sections and one short, inserted section. The Bargello strips in the left section line up with the lowest horizon lines; the bottom 3" of these strips is hidden by border strips. The Bargello strips in the center section line up with the highest horizon lines; the short section is inserted into this section. The Bargello strips in the right section line up with the middle horizon lines.

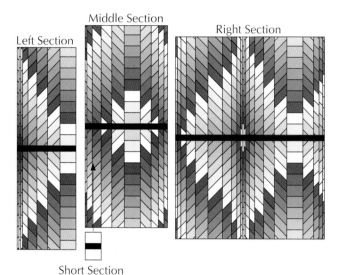

Left Section

Middle Section

Right Section

Short Section

1. Pin the backing to the batting. Draw 3 sets of horizon lines as shown.

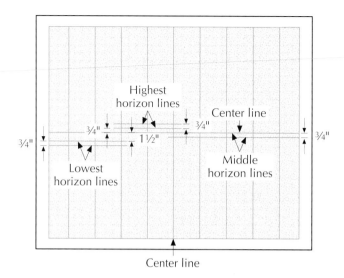

Highest horizon lines

Center line

¾" ¾"

¾" 1½" ¾"

Lowest horizon lines

Middle horizon lines

Center line

2. Beginning with the right section, cut loops for the top half of the quilt according to the diagram below. Separate straight loops into Bargello strips by removing the stitches between fabric segments. Cut across loops from up- and down-slanting tubes to make Bargello strips. Pin the strips onto your design wall. The strips from the straight tubes will be ½" longer than those from the slant tubes.

Cut width

¾" 1" 1¼" 1¾" 2¼" 2½" 1¾" 1¼" 1" ¾" ¾" 1" 1¼" 1¾" 2" 2¼" 2¾" 2" 1¼" 1" ¾"

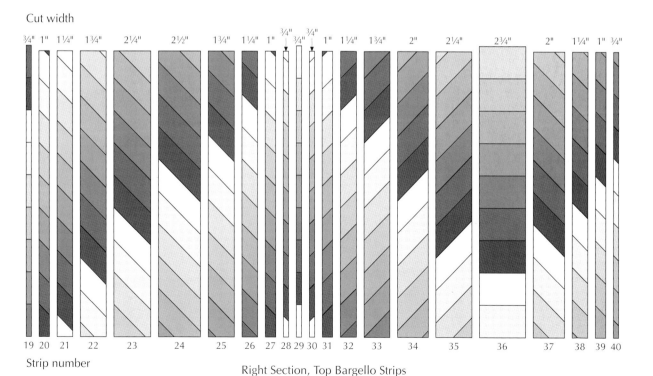

19 20 21 22 23 24 25 26 27 28 29 30 31 32 33 34 35 36 37 38 39 40

Strip number

Right Section, Top Bargello Strips

3. Cut loops for the bottom half of the section to mirror the top section. Open the loops and pin them in place on your design wall.

4. For the horizon segments, cut 2 strips, each 1¼" wide, from one of the fabrics. Cut the strips into segments to match the Bargello-strip widths. Join the top and bottom Bargello strips, with the horizon segments in between.

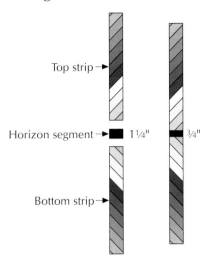

Top strip →

Horizon segment → ■ 1¼"   ■ ¾"

Bottom strip →

5. Place Strip 19 on the center line and place Strip 20 on top, right sides together, matching the horizon fabric with the middle horizon lines. Pin. Stitch, using a ¼"-wide seam allowance, along the right edges of the strips. Flip Strip 20 to the right and press as necessary.

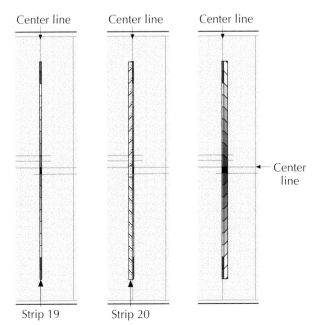

Center line   Center line   Center line

Center line

Strip 19   Strip 20

6. Continue sewing the Bargello strips to the quilt, working toward the right edge.

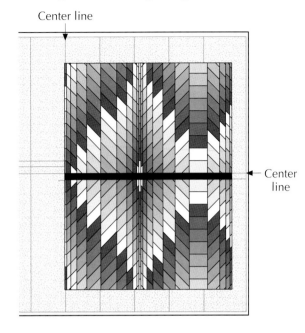

Center line

Center line

7. Prepare the Bargello strips for the middle section.

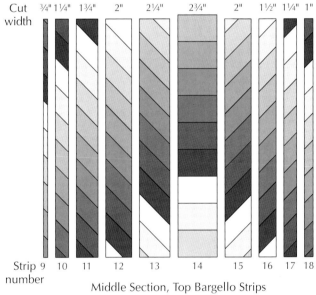

Cut width   ¾" 1¼" 1¾" 2" 2¼" 2¾" 2" 1½" 1¼" 1"

Strip number   9 10 11 12 13 14 15 16 17 18

Middle Section, Top Bargello Strips

8. Now lining up the horizon segments with the highest horizon lines, stitch Strip 18 to Strip 19. Continue sewing Bargello strips to the quilt, working from the center to the left edge until you have sewn Strip 12, flipped it to the left, and pinned it in place.

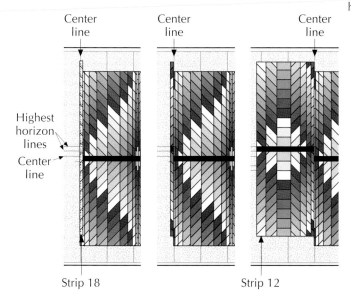

9. Cut 2 rectangles, each 2" x 2¾", from your lightest fabric and sew them to a 1¼" x 2¾" strip of horizon fabric. Finger-press a ¼"-wide seam allowance at the top and bottom edges. Place the section on Strip 12, right sides together, lining up the horizon segment with the lowest horizon lines. Pin in place.

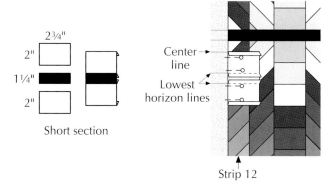

10. Continuing to use the highest horizon lines, pin and sew Strip 11, sewing the short section into the seam. Flip Strip 11 to the left, pin in place, and pin the short section out of the way.

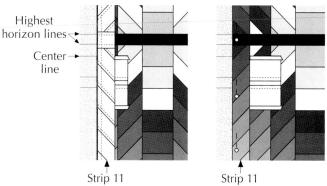

11. Sew, flip, and pin Strips 10 and 9. Now flip the short section to the left and hand stitch it to Strips 9, 10, and 11 along the folds, lining up the horizon segment with the lowest horizon lines on the batting.

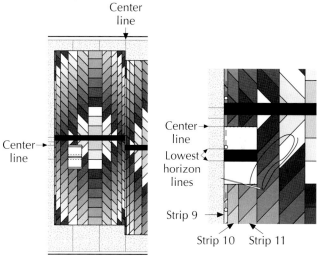

12. Prepare the Bargello strips for the left section.

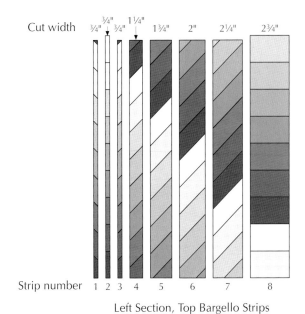

Cut width   ¾"   ¾"¾"   1¼"   1¾"   2"   2¼"   2¾"

Strip number   1   2   3   4   5   6   7   8

Left Section, Top Bargello Strips

13. Now lining up the horizon segments with the lowest horizon lines, stitch Strip 8 to Strip 9. Continue sewing Bargello strips to the quilt, working from the center to the left edge until you have sewn and flipped Strip 1.

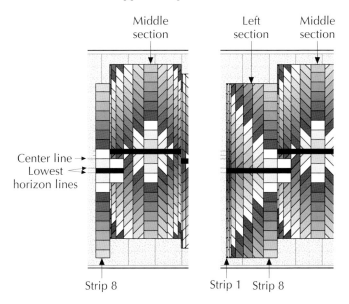

Middle section

Left section   Middle section

Center line
Lowest horizon lines

Strip 8   Strip 1   Strip 8

Borders and Binding

I designed the asymmetrical borders to fill in the uneven margins at the top and bottom of the Bargello areas. Use various strips of your remaining fabrics that complement the Bargello design. Follow the diagram below to add the border segments. Note that borders 2 and 10 cover up approximately 3" of Bargello strips in the far left section of the quilt. You may want to design your own borders, using mine only for inspiration.

Borders 1 through 5 and 8 are cut from the same fabric; borders 9, 10, and 11 from another; and borders 6, 7, and 12 from a third. You may desire a different selection of fabrics.

1. For border segments 1 through 5, cut 3 strips of fabric, each ¾" wide. Join the strips as needed and cut to the necessary lengths. Fold over ¼" at the right end of segments 1 and 2 and the left end of segment 3. Pin these strips to the quilt carefully, measuring up and down from the horizon lines to ensure parallel borders.

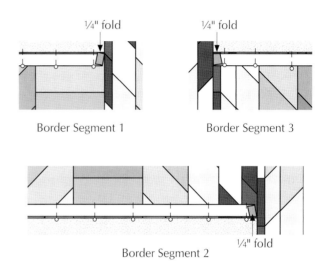

Border Segment 1   Border Segment 3

Border Segment 2

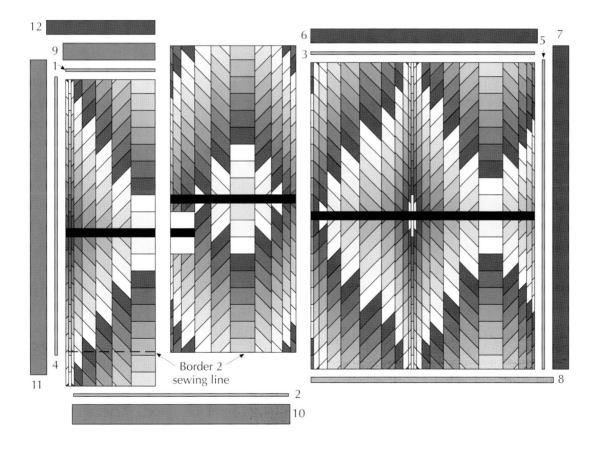

Border 2 sewing line

2. Stitch the border strips through all layers. Flip and pin. Hand stitch the folded ends of the strips to the Bargello strips they touch.

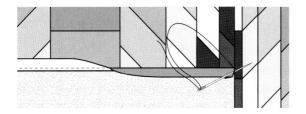

3. Pin and stitch border segments 4 and 5 to the sides of the quilt. Flip the strips and pin in place.
4. For border segment 6, cut 1 strip 1¾" wide. Fold over ¼" at the left end, pin, and stitch to the quilt. Flip the strip, pin, and hand stitch the folded end in place.
5. For border segment 7, cut 1 strip 2" wide. Pin and stitch the strip to the quilt. Flip the strip and pin in place.
6. For border segment 8, cut 1 strip 1" wide and follow the directions for border segment 6 (step 4).
7. For border segment 9, cut 1 strip 2" wide. Fold over ¼" at the right end, pin, and stitch to the quilt. Flip the strip out, pin, and hand stitch the end in place.
8. For border segment 10, cut 1 strip 2¼" wide and follow the directions for segment 9 (step 7).
9. For border segment 11, cut 1 strip 2" wide and follow the directions for segment 7 (step 5).
10. For border segment 12, cut 1 strip 1¾" wide and follow the directions for segment 9 (step 7).
11. Trim the batting and backing, leaving ½" extending beyond the edge of the outer border.
12. From the binding fabric, cut 4 strips, each 2" wide, for single-thickness binding. Join the ends with a 45° diagonal seam. Bind the quilt. The binding will measure ¾" wide when finished.

By Marge Edie, 1997, Clemson, South Carolina. This design says "celebration," with fold-out paper flowers, papier mâché, and silk dragons snaking through the excited crowd. Is it Mardi Gras in Rio or Chinese New Year?

This dynamic design is actually one curved design repeated three times, with minor changes. In the first repeat, Section A, the far left strip in the graph is omitted. In Section B, the two strips on the left and the two strips on the right are left out. And in Section C, the strip on the right is omitted. Because the changes occur at the edges, only one graph is required for the three sections. The design represented by the graph would make a beautiful wall piece by itself! For a wider quilt, put the omitted strips back into the design.

For a shorter quilt, cut the strips for the color runs a little narrower. If you subtract ⅛" from the width of each color-run strip, the quilt will measure approximately 7" shorter. If you subtract ¼", the quilt will measure 14" shorter. You can achieve a similar effect using fewer fabrics, but the flow of the design will change. I recommend rotating the loops on your design wall (see "Arranging Loops on Your Design Wall" on page 22) to audition any changes before cutting them into Bargello strips.

Materials: 42"-wide fabric

1⅛ yds. *each* of 13 fabrics for Bargello strips

7¼ yds. for backing

90" x 110" rectangle of batting

½ yd. for inner border

1¼ yds. for outer border

⅞ yd. for binding

Directions

Read the Bargello instructions on pages 10–28 before you begin and refer to them for each step in the quiltmaking process.

1. Cut 16 strips, each 2¼" wide, from each of the 13 fabrics for the Bargello strips. Sew 2 strips of each fabric together end to end to make a strip approximately 83½" long. Make a total of 8 long strips of each fabric.

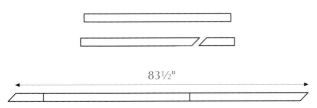

83½"

2. Using these long strips, construct 4 wide up-slanting color runs. Each strip will measure 1¾" wide when finished. The color run will measure approximately 23¼" across, from the lightest to the darkest strip, and 32⅞" on the diagonal edge.

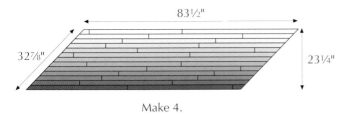

83½"

32⅞"

23¼"

Make 4.

3. Join 2 up-slanting color runs. Repeat for the other 2 up-slanting color runs. Join the color runs to make 2 up-slanting tubes.

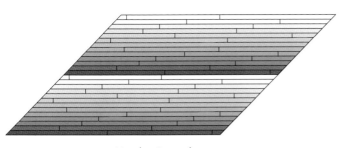

Up-slanting color runs
Make 2.

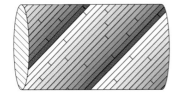

Up-slanting tubes
Make 2.

4. Make 2 down-slanting tubes in the same way.

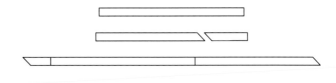

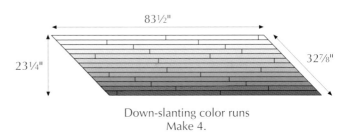

83½"

23¼"

32⅞"

Down-slanting color runs
Make 4.

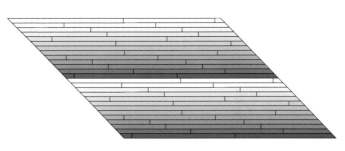

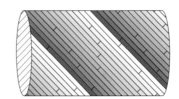

Down-slanting tubes
Make 2.

When the 4 tubes are folded flat, each will measure approximately 32⅛" from fold to fold and 60" long.

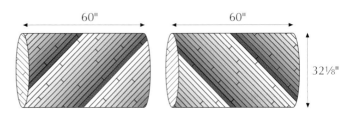

60"

60"

32⅛"

5. Refer to the graph and the Cutting Chart below for the placement and cut width of the Bargello strips. Cut the loops from the tubes using your standard quilter's ruler.

Strip No.	Cut Strip Width	Finished Strip Width
1	1¾"	1¼"
2	3½"	3"
3	1½"	1"
4	3"	2½"
5	1¼"	¾"
6	2½"	2"
7	1"	½"
8	1¾"	1¼"
9	1"	½"
10	1¼"	¾"
11	¾"	¼"
12	1"	½"
13	¾"	¼"

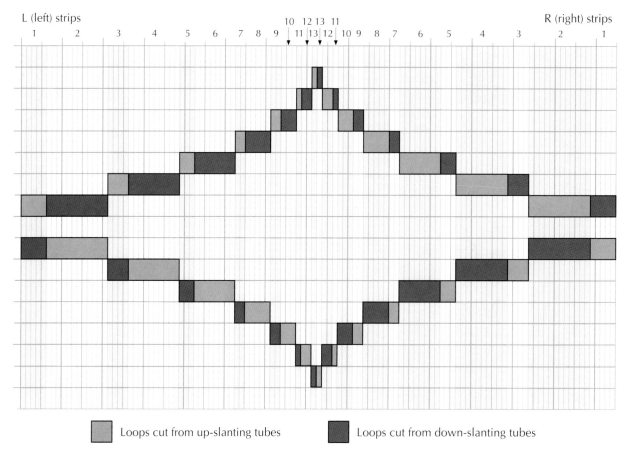

Loops cut from up-slanting tubes   Loops cut from down-slanting tubes

Section A uses Strips 2L through 13L, and 13R through 1R.
Section B uses Strips 3L through 13L, and 13R through 3R.
Section C uses Strips 1L through 13L, and 13R through 2R.

6. Separate the loops into Bargello strips, following the diagram below. Keep in mind that each tube is made up of 2 color runs; the strips shown are for above the horizon and include only 1 of the color-run repeats.

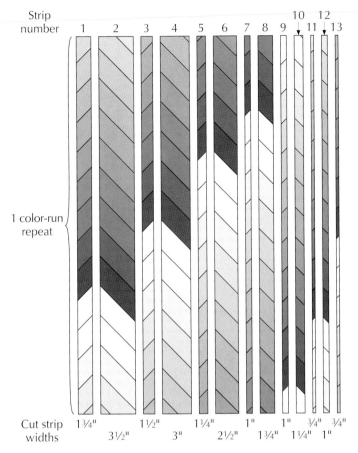

Above-horizon Bargello strips

Create the Bargello strips for below the horizon by cutting mirror-image loops that slant in the opposite direction.

7. Arrange the Bargello strips on your design wall. In both parts of Section A, the lower part of Section B, and the top part of Section C, each Bargello strip requires the entire loop cut from the tube. (Note that in Section A, the top and bottom parts of the Bargello strips will be trimmed or hidden by border and binding strips.)

For the top part of Section B, cut the Bargello strips in half and turn the second half upside down for the lower part of Section C. Cut lower portions of Strips 1L, 2L, and 2R to complete the strips in the lower part of Section C.

8. When the section you are working on is ready, sew the top Bargello strips to the bottom strips to create horizon seams.

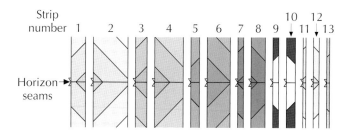

9. Cut the backing fabric as shown and piece a rectangle that measures approximately 92" x 111½".

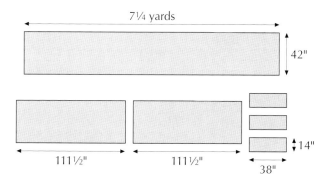

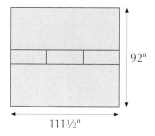

10. Layer the backing and batting. Draw 3 horizon lines as shown.

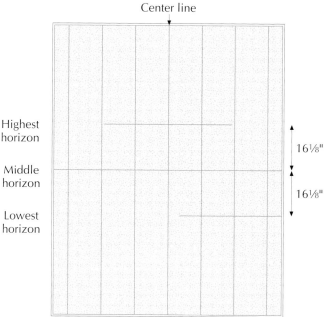

Assembling the Quilt

1. Begin with Section B. Align the horizon seam line in each Bargello strip with the highest horizon line on the batting. Place Strip 13R of Section B on the vertical center line and place Strip 12R on top, right sides together. Pin, then stitch, using a ¼"-wide seam allowance, along the right edges of the strips. Flip Strip 12R to the right, press as necessary, and pin in place.

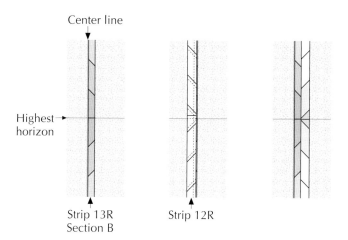

2. Continue sewing Section B strips to the quilt, working from the center to the right until Strip 3R is sewn down.

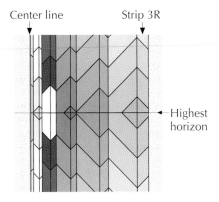

3. Stitch Section B Strip 13L to the left edge of Strip 13R. Continue sewing Section B strips to the quilt, working from the center to the left until Strip 3L of Section B is sewn down.

4. Continue construction with strips from Section C. Line up the horizon seam in each strip with the lowest horizon line on the batting. Place Strip 1L on the right edge of Section B, right sides together. Pin, then stitch, using a ¼"-wide seam allowance, along the right edges of the strips. Flip Strip 1L to the right, press as necessary, and pin in place.

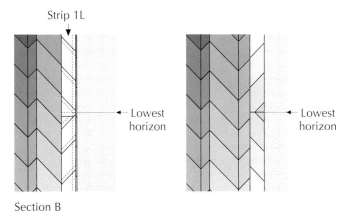

5. Continue sewing strips to the quilt, working to the right edge until Strip 2R of Section C is sewn down.

6. Continue construction with strips from Section A. Line up the horizon seam in each strip with the middle horizon line on the batting. Place Strip 1R on the left edge of Section B, right sides together. If desired, trim the excess strip at the top and bottom, leaving enough to be covered by borders and binding. Pin, then stitch, using a ¼"-wide seam allowance, along the left edges of the strips. Flip Strip 1R to the left, press as necessary, and pin in place.

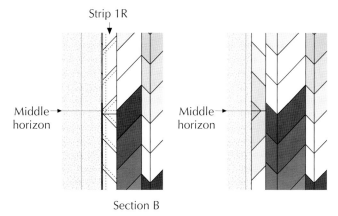

Section B

7. Continue sewing strips to the quilt, working to the left edge until Strip 2L of Section A is sewn down.

Section A   Section B   Section C

Borders and Binding

1. From the inner border fabric, cut 10 strips, each 1½" wide. Join the strips as needed. Sew the side inner borders to the quilt; then add the top and bottom inner borders. The border will measure 1" when finished.

2. From the outer border fabric, cut 10 strips, each 4" wide. Join the strips as needed. Sew the outer borders to the quilt, following the directions in step 1. The border will measure 3½" wide when finished.

3. Trim the batting and backing, leaving ½" extending beyond the edge of the outer border.

4. From the binding fabric, cut 11 strips, each 2" wide, for single-thickness binding. Join the ends with a 45° diagonal seam. Bind the quilt. The binding will measure ¾" wide when finished.

Vail

FINISHED SIZE: 29" X 39½"

By Marge Edie, 1997, Clemson, South Carolina. The bold geometry in "Kansas," my first experiment with slant Bargello, is polished up a bit for this design variation. The icy colors and steep curves made me think of a cold day of downhill skiing.

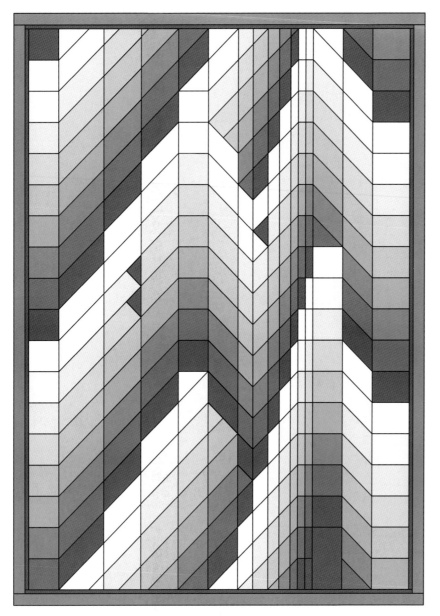

*T*he sweep of this design reminds me of glaciers, downhill skiing, and ice—all too harsh and too cold for my blood. We quilters are content to create the danger of the great outdoors with fabric and color. Although I matched the seams carefully, it isn't necessary; the quilt will still have interesting movement, perhaps even a devil-may-care feeling. This mood may reflect the stark difference between Vail and our prairie lands.

Complications in this design can arise if the slant color runs are not quite 45° angles, because the slope may increase or decrease faster or slower than predicted. In fact, I had to straighten the top and bottom edges in "Vail" with the first border strips to keep the quilt from becoming a parallelogram. That's why the top and bottom edges of the quilt in the photo are not exactly as laid out in the pattern.

Before you cut your loops into Bargello strips, carefully pin them onto your design wall to best predict where to make the separation: it may differ a bit from the pattern indications. I cut my strips exactly as shown in the illustrations, and the bottom and top edges had to be corrected about ¼" from side to side.

Materials: 42"-wide fabric

⅜ yd. *each* of 9 fabrics for Bargello strips

1 yd. for backing

33" x 44" rectangle of batting

⅛ yd. for inner border

¼ yd. for outer border

¼ yd. for binding

Directions

Read the Bargello instructions on pages 10–28 before you begin and refer to them for each step in the quiltmaking process.

1. Cut 1 strip, 2½" wide, from each of the 9 fabrics for the Bargello strips. Construct 1 straight color run. The strips will measure 2" wide when finished, and the color run will measure 18½" wide. Press the seams toward the light fabrics.

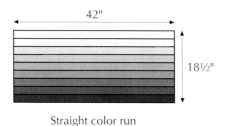

Straight color run

2. Cut the color run in half. Sew the sections together to make 1 half-width tube.

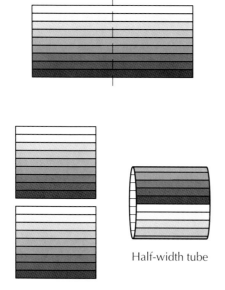

Half-width tube

3. Cut 3 strips from each of the 9 fabrics using the Bias Stripper ruler at the 2" mark; each strip will measure approximately 1⅞" wide.

4. Construct 1 down-slanting color run. The color run will measure approximately 13¼" across, from the lightest to the darkest strip, and 18¾" on the diagonal. Cut the color run in half on the 45° diagonal. Sew the sections together to make 1 half-width tube.

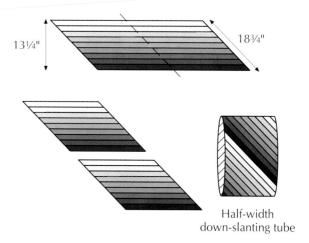

Half-width
down-slanting tube

5. Sew the remaining strips into 2 up-slanting color runs. Sew the color runs together to make 1 tube.

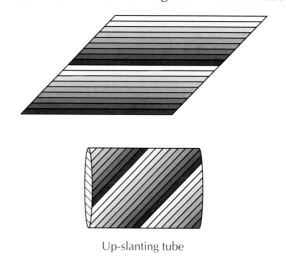

Up-slanting tube

When the 3 tubes are folded flat, they will measure approximately 18" from fold to fold.

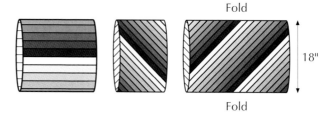

Fold

18"

Fold

6. Refer to the Cutting Chart below and the photo on page 63 for the placement and cut width of the Bargello strips. Starting in the middle with Strip 8, cut loops from the 3 tubes using your standard quilter's ruler.

Cut from Straight Tube

Strip No.	No. of Strips per Set	Cut Strip Width	Finished Strip Width
12, 13	2	1"	½"
1, 5, 14	2	2½"	2"
16	1	3"	2½"

Cut from Up-Slanting Tube

Strip No.	No. of Strips per Set	Cut Strip Width	Finished Strip Width
11	1	1"	½"
9, 10	2	1¼"	¾"
7, 8	2	1½"	1"
5, 6	2	2½"	2"
3, 4	2	3"	2½"
2	1	3½"	3"

Cut from Down-Slanting Tube

Strip No.	No. of Strips per Set	Cut Strip Width	Finished Strip Width
7	1	1½"	1"
6, 14, 15	3	2½"	2"

7. Separate or cut the loops as shown below, leaving any excess fabric at the top or bottom edges in case of error. Working from the center, arrange the loops and loop segments on your design wall. Using the diagrams at the bottom of the page, cut the extra triangles, rectangles, and quadrilaterals from leftover tubes or fabric and pin them in place where they occur in the Bargello strips.

Strip number
1 2 3 4 5 6 7 8 9 10 11 12 13 14 15 16

2½" 3½" 3" 3" 2½" 2½" 1½" 1¼" 1" 2½" 3"
1½" 1¼" 1" 1" 2½"

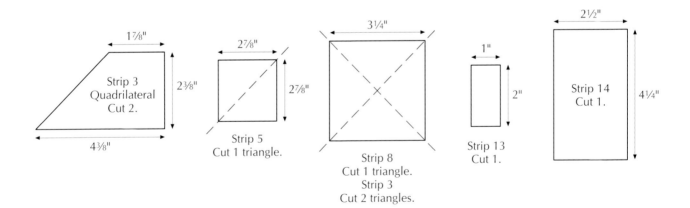

1⅞"
Strip 3 Quadrilateral Cut 2.
2⅜"
4⅜"

2⅞"
Strip 5 Cut 1 triangle.
2⅞"

3¼"
Strip 8 Cut 1 triangle.
Strip 3 Cut 2 triangles.

1"
Strip 13 Cut 1.
2"

2½"
Strip 14 Cut 1.
4¼"

Join the partial strips and extra pieces to make complete Bargello strips.

8. Prepare the backing and batting.

9. Place Strip 6 on the center line and place Strip 7 on top, right sides together. Pin, then stitch, using a ¼"-wide seam allowance, along the right edges of the strips. Flip Strip 7 to the right and press as necessary. Continue sewing strips to the quilt, working from the center to the right edge.

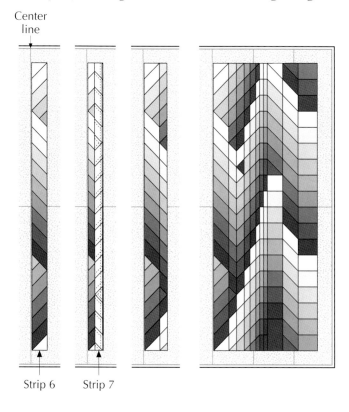

Center line

Strip 6   Strip 7

10. Stitch Strip 5 to Strip 6 on the left edge. Continue sewing strips to the quilt, working from the center to the left edge.

Borders and Binding

1. From the inner border fabric, cut 4 strips, each ¾" wide. Sew the side borders to the quilt; then add the top and bottom borders. The border will measure ¼" wide when finished.

2. From the outer border fabric, cut 4 strips, each 1¼" wide. Pin the borders to the quilt and stitch from the back; see the Tip on page 25. The border will measure ¾" when finished.

3. Trim the batting and backing, leaving ½" extending beyond the edge of the outer border.

4. From the binding fabric, cut 4 strips, each 2" wide, for single-thickness binding. Join the ends with a 45° diagonal seam. Bind the quilt. The binding will measure ¾" wide when finished.

Covenant

FINISHED SIZE: 46½" x 37½"

By Marge Edie, 1996, Clemson, South Carolina. Soft, rainbow pastels, combined with a radiating design, reminded me of the promise to Noah from the heavens that there would never again be a flood of such destruction. A friend says she sees a dove in the background.

"*Covenant*" is different from the other patterns in this book in that it is set on the diagonal. Because this design uses only slant Bargello strips, you can use a standard quilter's ruler for measuring and cutting. You can make "Hawk" (see page 90) just like "Covenant" by substituting solid background strips for the lower corners' Bargello designs.

Materials: 42"-wide fabric

¼ yd. *each* of 9 fabrics (darker pastels)
for Bargello strips

¼ yd. *each* of 9 fabrics (lighter pastels)
for Bargello strips

¼ yd. *each* of the 2 lightest fabrics for extra strips
and triangles in Bargello strips

1½ yds. for backing

51" x 42" rectangle of batting

¼ yd. for border

½ yd. for binding

Directions

Read the Bargello instructions on pages 10–28 before you begin and refer to them for each step in the quiltmaking process.

1. Cut 4 strips, each 1¾" wide, from each of the 18 fabrics for the Bargello strips. Sew 2 strips of each fabric together end to end to make a strip approximately 83½" long. Make 2 long strips of each fabric.

2. Construct 1 up-slanting and 1 down-slanting color run from the lighter pastel group. Do the same for the darker pastel group. The strips will measure 1¼" wide when finished. The color runs will measure 11¾" across and 16⅝" on the diagonal edge. Press the seams toward the light fabrics.

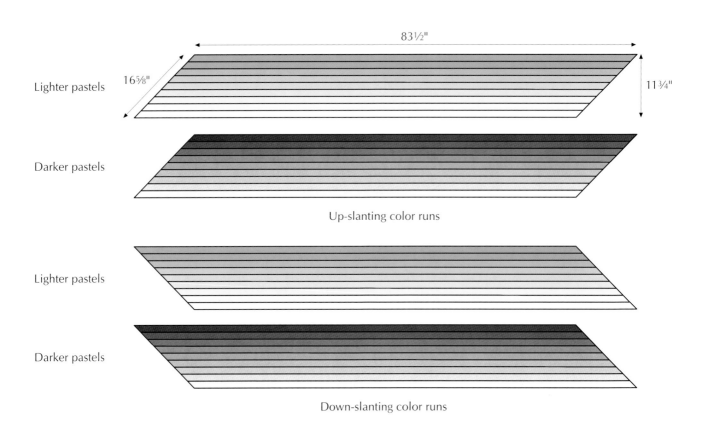

Lighter pastels   16⅝"   83½"   11¾"

Darker pastels

Up-slanting color runs

Lighter pastels

Darker pastels

Down-slanting color runs

3. Refer to the diagram and the Cutting Charts below for the placement and cut width of the Bargello strip segments.

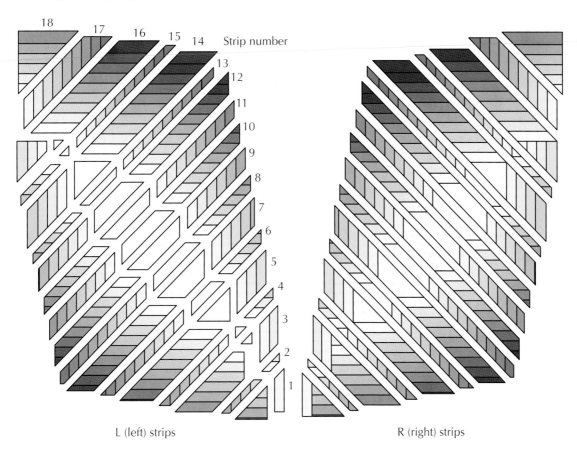

L (left) strips   R (right) strips

Cut one from each color run.

Strip No.	Cut Strip Width	Finished Strip Width
2	1¼"	¾"
3	3⅞"	3⅜"
4	1½"	1"
5	3½"	3"
6	1¾"	1¼"
7	3"	2½"
8	1⅞"	1⅜"
9	2⅜"	1⅞"
10	2¼"	1¾"
11	2"	1½"
12	2½"	2"
13	1⅜"	⅞"
14	3⅞"	3⅜"
15	1⅜"	⅞"
16	4⅛"	3⅝"

Cut one *each* from the dark up-slanting and the dark down-slanting color runs.

Strip No.	Cut Strip Width	Finished Strip Width
1	3¼"	2¾"
18	5¾"	5¼"

Cut one *each* from the light up-slanting and the light down-slanting color runs.

Strip No.	Cut Strip Width	Finished Strip Width
17	3⅛"	2⅝"

4. Follow the diagrams below to draw and cut the extra trapezoids and triangles from the lighter fabrics. Use scraps of your darkest fabrics to create fill-in pieces at the tops of rows 12 and 14. Join the segments and pieces to make the Bargello strips.

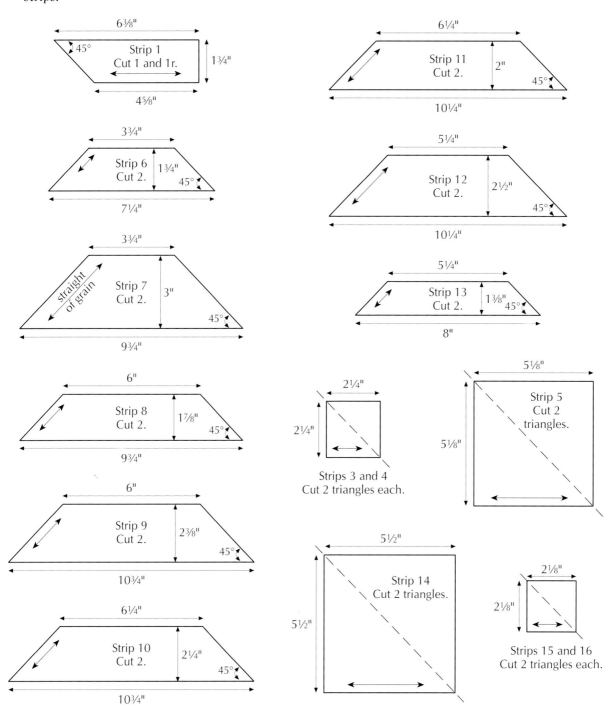

All measurements indicate cut sizes.

Do not remove excess fabric from the ends of the partial Bargello strips as you join them with other pieces to make complete Bargello strips. Trim the ends as you sew the strips to the backing and batting—just in case the strips don't quite cover the Bargello area.

Note that strips cut from the darker pastel color run are sewn at one end of each Bargello strip, and strips from the lighter pastels at the other.

5. Pin the batting to the backing. Draw a rectangle approximately 45" by 35¼" for the design area; draw a vertical line down the center.

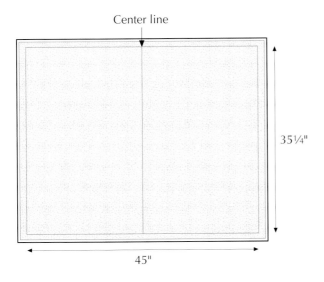

Using your quilter's ruler, draw a 45° diagonal line through each half of the rectangle, starting at the top of the center line, as shown. Use your ruler to draw more diagonal lines for strip placement check-ups.

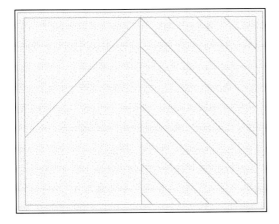

Draw 2 triangles, 6" on each short side, at the lower center of your design area.

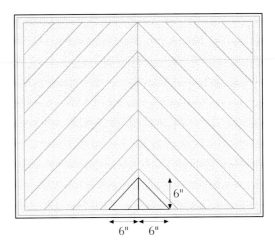

6. Place Strip 1L (1 left) along the diagonal edge of the left triangle you just drew, overlapping the center line by ¼" and allowing some of the strip to extend below the lower marked line. Trim the strip 1½" below the lower line. (The borders and binding will cover up this extra bit of strip.)

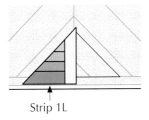

Strip 1L

7. Fold under ¼" on the long vertical edge of Strip 1R. Place it along the diagonal edge of the lower right triangle, with the fold on the center vertical line, and pin in place. Blindstitch the folded edge to Strip 1L on the center line.

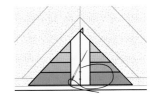

Blindstitch the fold to strip 1L.

8. With right sides together, pin Strip 2L to Strip 1L. Stitch, using a ¼"-wide seam allowance, along the edges of the strips. Flip Strip 2L, press as necessary, and pin in place.

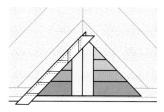

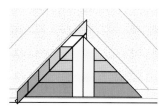

9. Pin Strip 2R in place and stitch to Strip 1R, *beginning the seam at the center vertical line.* Turn the upper end of the strip down ¼", forming a horizontal fold as shown; trim the end as necessary.

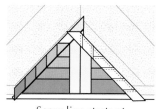

Seam line starts at
center vertical line.

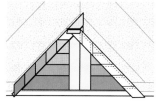

Fold down ¼".

Flip the strip, pin, and blindstitch the folded edge to Strip 2L on the center line.

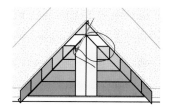

Flip strip and blindstitch.

10. Continue sewing the Bargello strips up the quilt, keeping the seams lined up as precisely as possible. As you place each strip, trim the end to overlap the center line ¼"; then fold under the end and blindstitch the folded edge to the center line.

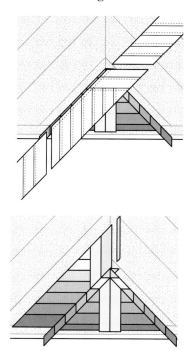

As you add the Bargello strips, keep the center vertical line straight and the left and right sides balanced. Check the strip alignment against the diagonal pencil lines as you stitch and flip the strips, making adjustments as necessary.

Borders and Binding

1. From the border fabric, cut 4 strips, each 1" wide. Join the strips as needed. Sew the side borders to the quilt; then add the top and bottom borders. The border will measure ½" when finished.
2. Trim the batting and backing, leaving ¾" extending beyond the edge of the outer border.
3. From the binding fabric, cut 5 strips, each 2½" wide, for single-thickness binding. Join the ends with a 45° diagonal seam. Bind the quilt. The binding will measure 1" wide when finished.

St. Elmo's Fire

FINISHED SIZE: 33¼" x 51¼"

By Marge Edie, 1996, Clemson, South Carolina. This piece snaps with energy, a result of the movement in the design and the force of the colors. I tried to create a Bargello background, but soon realized that the design was more powerful with near-solid pieces behind the floating streak.

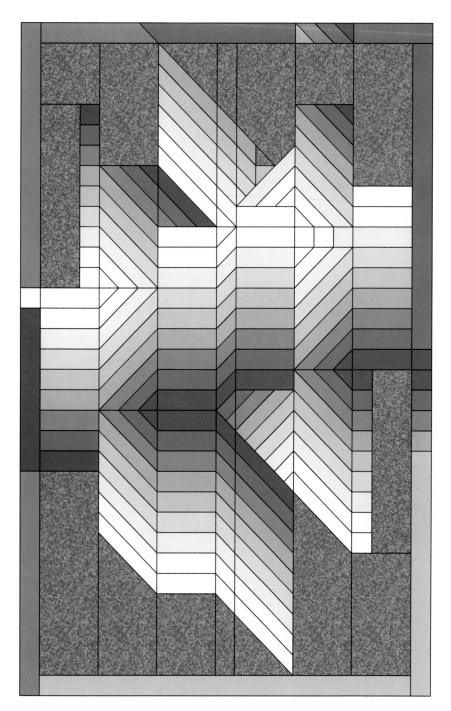

*This design started as an experi-
ment without borders. It reminds
me of a streak of loose electrical
current across the air, but if made
in more subtle colors, it could
easily resemble wind. I tried various ways to fill in what are now
the background areas with more
Bargello but finally realized that the
design was stronger when floating
on a solid field. The effect will
change if you select a background
fabric that is dramatically different
from the color-run fabrics.*

Materials:
42"-wide fabric

¼ yd. *each* of 9 fabrics for
Bargello strips

⅝ yd. of background fabric

1½ yds. for backing

38" x 56" rectangle of batting

¼ yd. *each* of 3 fabrics for border

⅜ yd. for binding

Directions

Read the Bargello instructions on pages 10–28 before you begin and refer to them for each step in the quiltmaking process.

1. Cut 1 strip, 2" wide, from each of the 9 fabrics for the Bargello strips. Construct 1 straight color run. The strips will measure 1½" wide when finished, and the color run will measure 14" wide. Press the seams toward the light fabrics.

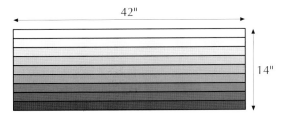

Straight color run

2. Cut 3 strips from each of the 9 fabrics using the Bias Stripper ruler at the 1½" mark; each strip will measure approximately 1½" wide. Construct 1 up-slanting color run and 2 down-slanting color runs. The strips will measure approximately 1" wide when finished. The color runs will measure approximately 10" across, from the lightest to the darkest strips, and 14" on the diagonal edge.

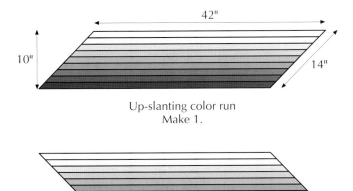

Up-slanting color run
Make 1.

Down-slanting color run
Make 2.

3. Refer to the Cutting Chart below for the placement and cut width of the Bargello strips. Cut the strips from the 3 types of color runs.

Cut from Straight Color Run

Strip No.	No. of Strips	Cut Strip Width	Finished Strip Width
1, 3, 5, 7	5	5"	4½"
1, 6 (reserve part for right-hand border segment), 7	3	2"	1½"

Cut from Up-Slanting Color Run

Strip No.	No. of Strips	Cut Strip Width	Finished Strip Width
2, 5, 6	4	5"	4½"
4, left-hand border segment	2	2"	1½"

Use leftovers for triangle shapes in strips 4 and 5.

Cut from Down-Slanting Color Run

Strip No.	No. of Strips	Cut Strip Width	Finished Strip Width
2, 3, 5, 6	6	5"	4½"
4, 5	3	2"	1½"

4. Trim the slant strips according to the diagrams below. Use your Bias Stripper ruler or standard ruler to cut the 45° angles. Be sure to leave a ¼" seam allowance at the top, bottom, or angled edge of each strip you trim.

Strip segments in Strips 2 and 6

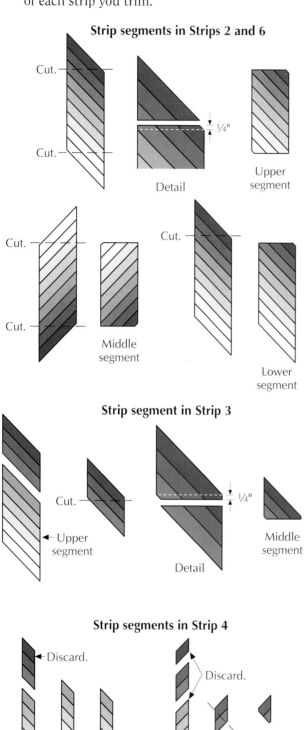

Strip segment in Strip 3

Strip segments in Strip 4

Strip segment in Strip 5

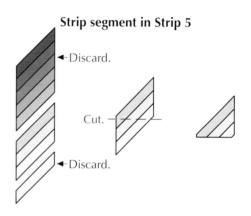

Four-sided piece in Strip 5

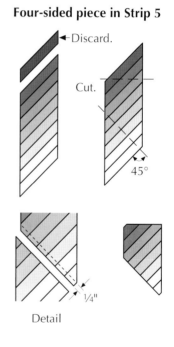

Strip segment in Strip 5

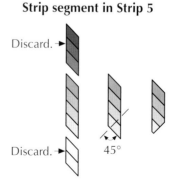

5. Cut triangles, quadrilaterals, and polygon J from the background fabric according to the diagrams below.

6. Arrange the strip segments on your design wall as you cut them from the color runs and background fabric.

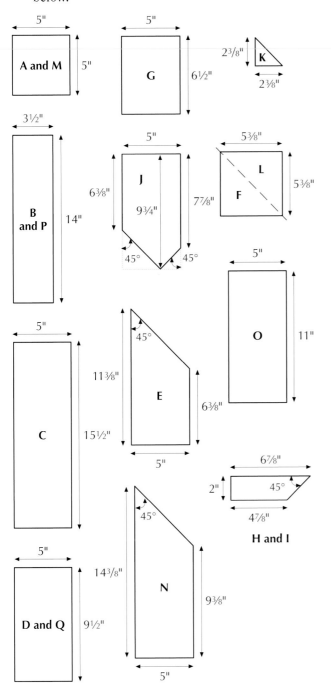

A and M — 5", 5"

G — 5", 6½"

K — 2⅜", 2⅜"

B and P — 3½", 14"

J — 5", 6⅜", 9¾", 45°, 45°

F / L — 5⅜", 5⅜", 7⅞"

C — 5", 15½"

E — 45°, 11⅜", 6⅜", 5"

O — 5", 11"

D and Q — 5", 9½", 14⅜"

N — 45°, 14⅜", 9⅜", 5"

H and I — 6⅞", 2", 45°, 4⅞"

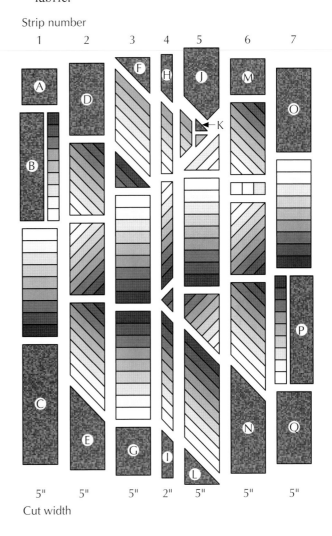

Strip number

1   2   3   4   5   6   7

A D F H J M O
B
C E G I L N P Q
K

5"   5"   5"   2"   5"   5"   5"

Cut width

Join the strips and pieces to make complete Bargello strips.

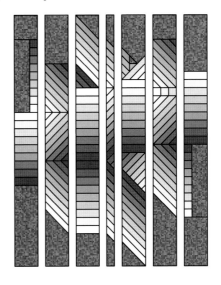

7. Prepare the backing and batting.
8. Place Strip 4 on the center line and place Strip 5 on top, right sides together. Pin, matching the seams between strips. Stitch, using a ¼"-wide seam allowance, along the right edges of the strips. Flip Strip 5 to the right and press as necessary. Continue sewing strips to the quilt, working from the center to the right edge.

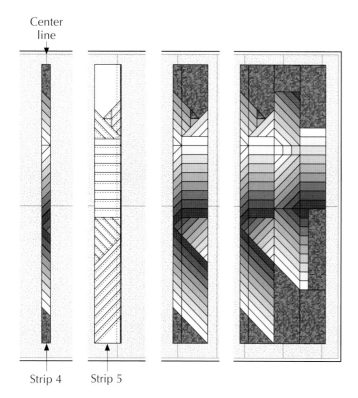

Center line

Strip 4   Strip 5

9. Stitch Strip 3 to Strip 4. Continue sewing strips to the quilt, working from the center to the left edge.

Borders and Binding

1. From the border fabrics and remaining straight and slant color runs, cut strips as shown below, each 2" wide. Join the border segments. Sew the bottom border to the quilt, then, in order, the right border, top border, and left border.

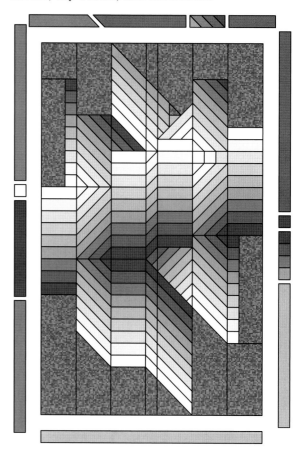

2. Trim the batting and backing, leaving ⅝" extending beyond the edge of the border.
3. From the binding fabric, cut 4 strips, each 2¼" wide, for single-thickness binding. Join the ends with a 45° diagonal seam. Bind the quilt. The binding will measure ⅞" wide when finished.

Crystal City
FINISHED SIZE: 32¾" X 49"

By Marge Edie, 1995, Clemson, South Carolina. My second slant Bargello project has a strong architectural feeling, accentuated by fabrics that suggest dimension.

*W*hen I completed this design, it reminded me of the magic environment Superman created in the frozen North by slinging a crystal into the ice. It also looks like the suburb of the same name in Washington, D.C., with its many glass office buildings and greenways.

Some Bargello strips in this quilt are portions of strips cut from the color runs. Be sure to save the leftover segments, just in case you want to insert portions into other Bargello strips. This substitution gives the design its interwoven appearance.

"Crystal City" requires a certain amount of precision in cutting and sewing. But don't look too closely at the photo: it has plenty of points that don't come close to meeting, yet it's still a lovely piece to live with.

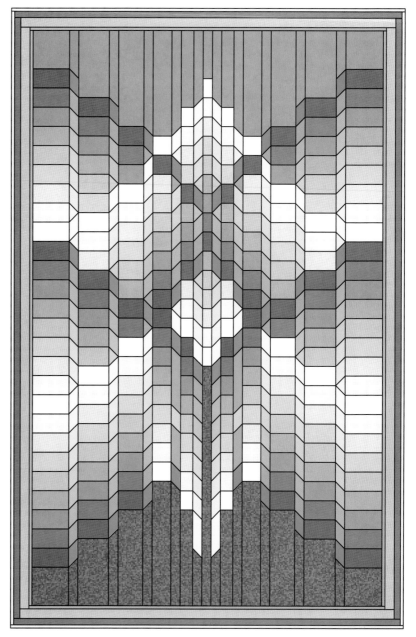

Materials: 42"-wide fabric

¼ yd. *each* of 9 fabrics in bright tones for Bargello strips

¼ yd. *each* of 9 corresponding fabrics in slightly duller, darker tones for Bargello strips

½ yd. *each* of 2 fabrics for top and bottom background pieces (These may be the same fabrics as in the color runs.)

1½ yds. for backing

38" x 53" rectangle of batting

¼ yd. *each* for borders 1, 2, 3, and 4

¼ yd. for binding

Directions

Read the Bargello instructions on pages 10–28 before you begin and refer to them for each step in the quiltmaking process.

1. Cut 2 strips, each 2" wide, from each fabric in the brighter group. Construct 2 straight color runs. The strips will measure 1½" wide when finished, and the color run will measure 14" wide. Press the seams toward the light fabrics.

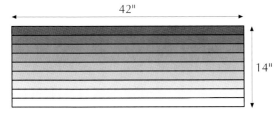

Straight color run
Make 2.

Cut 1 additional 2"-wide strip from the darkest fabric in this group for the substitution squares in strips 7L and 7R, and rectangles in strips 9L and 9R. (You'll need to trim the strip to 1½" wide for the pieces in strips 9L and 9R.)

2. Cut 2 strips from each fabric in the darker, duller group using the Bias Stripper ruler at the 1½" mark; each strip will measure slightly more than 1½" wide.

3. Construct 1 up-slanting color run and 1 down-slanting color run. The strips will measure slightly more than 1" wide when finished. The color runs will measure approximately 10" across, from the lightest to the darkest strip, and 14" on the diagonal edge.

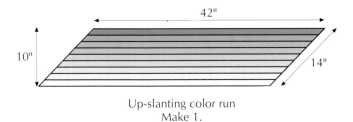

Up-slanting color run
Make 1.

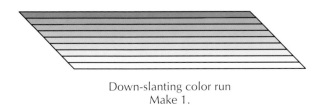

Down-slanting color run
Make 1.

Cut 1 additional strip, using the 1½" mark on the Bias Stripper ruler, from the darkest fabric in this group for the small substitution parallelograms in strips 6L, 6R, 8L, 8R, 10L, and 10R.

4. Refer to the Cutting Chart below to cut Bargello strips from the 3 types of color runs.

Cut from Straight Color Runs

Strip	Number of Strips	Cut Strip Width	Finished Strip Width
1L, 1R	6	3½"	3"
3L, 3R	6	3"	2½"
5L, 5R	6	2½"	2"
7L, 7R	4	2"	1½"
9L, 9R	6	1½"	¾"
11	2	1¼"	¾"

Cut from Up-Slanting Color Run

Strip	Number of Strips	Cut Strip Width	Finished Strip Width
2L	1	1¼"	¾"
4L	2	1¼"	¾"
6L	2	1¼"	¾"
8L	1	1¼"	¾"
10L	1	1¼"	¾"
2R	2	1¼"	¾"
4R	2	1¼"	¾"
10R	2	1¼"	¾"

Cut from Down-Slanting Color Run

Strip	Number of Strips	Cut Strip Width	Finished Strip Width
2L	2	1¼"	¾"
4L	2	1¼"	¾"
10L	2	1¼"	¾"
2R	1	1¼"	¾"
4R	2	1¼"	¾"
6R	2	1¼"	¾"
8R	1	1¼"	¾"
10R	1	1¼"	¾"

5. Following the diagram below, remove unneeded
fabric pieces from the Bargello strips to make the
required segments, reserving some pieces to insert in other locations. Use these removed pieces
as patterns to cut replacement squares, rectangles,
and parallelograms from the extra strips of dark
fabrics.

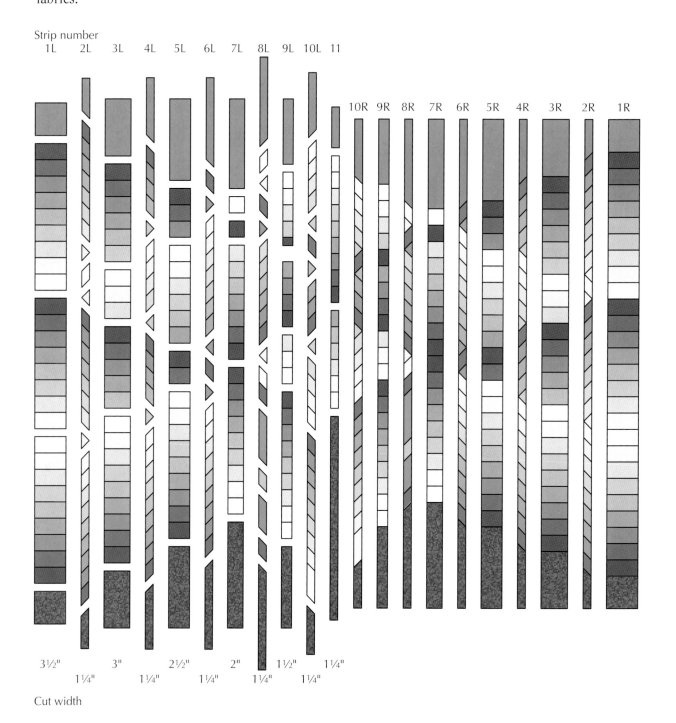

6. Draw the pattern pieces below and cut the background pieces from the 2 background fabrics. Trim the rectangle ends on a 45° angle as shown for Strips 2, 4, 6, 8, and 10.

Top background
For even-numbered rows, cut 1 and 1 reversed.
For odd-numbered rows, cut 2 each, except for row 11; cut 1.

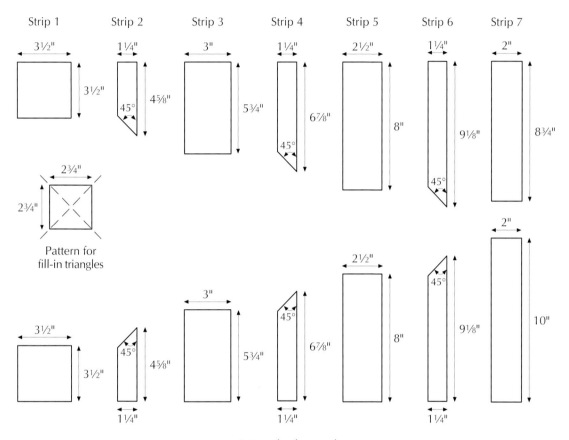

Pattern for
fill-in triangles

Bottom background
For even-numbered rows, cut 1 and 1 reversed.
For odd-numbered rows, cut 2 each, except for row 11; cut 1.

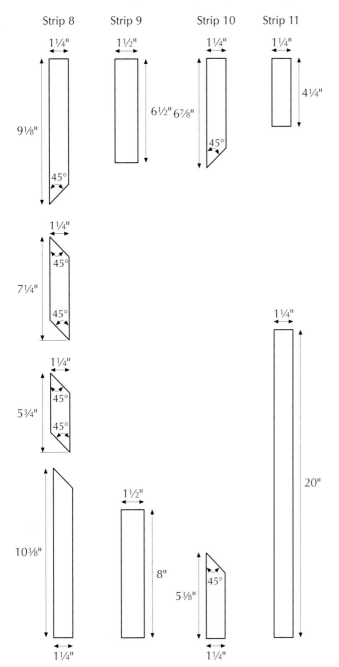

Top background
For even-numbered rows, cut 1 and 1 reversed.
For odd-numbered rows, cut 2 each, except for row 11; cut 1.

Strip 8   Strip 9   Strip 10   Strip 11

1¼"   1½"   1¼"   1¼"

9⅛"

45°

6½" 6⅞"

4¼"

45°

1¼"

45°

7¼"

45°

1¼"

45°

5¾"

45°

1¼"

1¼"

10⅜"

1½"

8"

5⅜"

45°

20"

1¼"   1¼"

Bottom background
For even-numbered rows, cut 1 and 1 reversed.
For odd-numbered rows, cut 2 each, except for row 11; cut 1.

7. Arrange the Bargello strip segments, substitution pieces, and background pieces on your design wall in strips. Join the segments and pieces to make the Bargello strips.

8. Prepare the backing and batting.

9. Place Strip 11 along the center line and place Strip 10R on top, right sides together, matching seams and triangle points. Pin, then stitch, using a ¼"-wide seam allowance, along the right edges of the strips. Flip Strip 10R to the right and press as necessary.

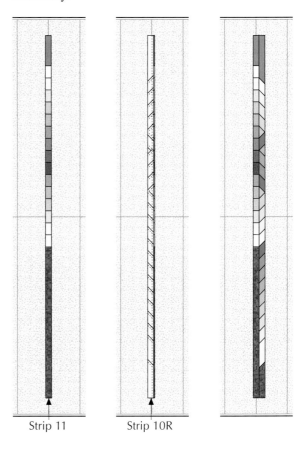

Strip 11   Strip 10R

10. Continue sewing strips to the quilt, working from the center to the right edge.
11. Return to the center and stitch Strip 10L to Strip 11. Continue sewing strips to the quilt, working from the center to the left edge.

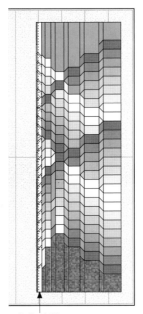 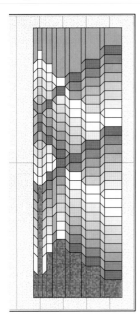

Strip 10L

Borders and Binding

1. From border 1 fabric, cut 5 strips, each ¾" wide. Join strips as needed. Sew the side borders to the quilt; then add the top and bottom borders. The border will measure ¼" when finished.
2. From border 2 fabric, cut 5 strips, each 1¼" wide. Join the strips as needed. Pin borders to the quilt and stitch from the back as directed in the Tip on page 25. The border will measure ¾" when finished.
3. From border 3 fabric, cut 5 strips, each 1" wide. Join the strips as needed and attach, following the directions in step 1. The border will measure ½" when finished.
4. From border 4 fabric, cut 5 strips, each ¾" wide. Join the strips as needed and attach, following the directions in step 1. The border will measure ¼" when finished.
5. Trim the batting and backing, leaving ¼" extending beyond the edge of the outer border.
6. From the binding fabric, cut 5 strips, each 1½" wide, for single-thickness binding. Join the ends with a 45° diagonal seam. Bind the quilt. The binding will measure ½" wide when finished.

GALLERY

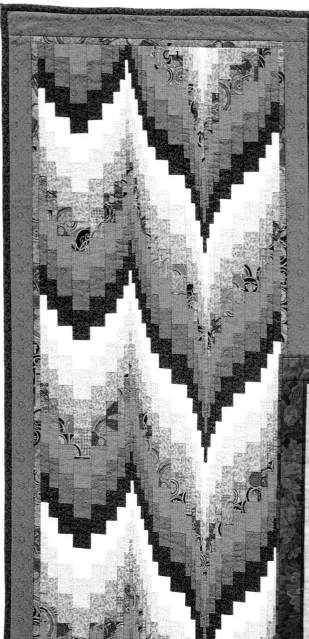

SEA BREEZE

By Lori Kuba, 1993, Seneca, South Carolina, 28" x 57½". Lori selected fabrics to match carpeting, wallpaper, and artwork in a hallway leading to her bedrooms. This piece was her first Bargello quilt—a project in my beginner class—and is a wonderful example of traditional Bargello.

A PEACH RUNS THROUGH IT

By Gale Pemberton, 1997, Salem, South Carolina, 28" x 36½". Gale agreed to test my pattern with a softer set of colors. Her fabric choices convey the gentle coloration and natural forms of seashells and seashore. A more elaborate border treatment softens the geometry of the Bargello design.

Tidal Pool II

By Marge Edie, 1997, Clemson, South Carolina, 25" x 32½". In this variation of "Tidal Pool," I used darker, duller fabrics for the slant color runs to create a three-dimensional illusion. See page 40 for the first version of the design.

Tidal Pool III

By Marge Edie, 1997, Clemson, South Carolina, 25" x 32½". Substituting quarter-inch separator strips for part of each straight-Bargello strip adds to the interest and softens the geometry.

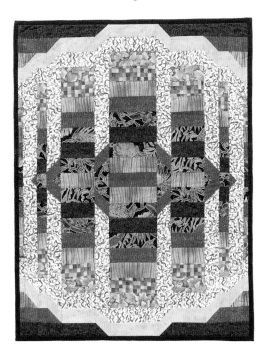

Tidal Pool IV

By Marge Edie, 1997, Clemson, South Carolina, 25" x 32½". Using only one fabric for the slant color runs dramatically changes the design and its color proportions.

Tidal Pool V

By Marge Edie, 1997, Clemson, South Carolina, 25" x 32½". I cut all of the background segments out of the darkest fabric and reversed the order of the color-run segments to create a zigzag, zipper-tooth design.

Hawk

By Marge Edie, 1996, Clemson, South Carolina, 47" x 38". The geometry is the same as in "Covenant" (page 68), except that I substituted solid-fabric strips for the Bargello strips in the lower corners. I see the wings of a raptor outspread and soaring.

Rainy Day at Pine Lake

By Marge Edie, 1996, Clemson, South Carolina, 47" x 30". To suggest the reflecting edge of a creek or pond, I placed a few strips of the bright fabrics used above the water line among the duller strips below.

O CANADA

By Ann Hawkins, 1997,
Seneca, South Carolina,
52½" x 39". Ann graciously
agreed to test my pattern,
using fall colors, in a quilt
that now adorns her living
room wall. Ann's wonderful
combination of prints
creates sparkle in the
design.

CHRYSANTHEMUM

By Marge Edie, 1997,
Clemson, South Carolina,
58½" x 43½". I see unfold-
ing, spiky petals in this
geometry, while one of my
friends sees the pages of a
book. But, with pinks and
plums, it had to be flowers.
The pattern is related to
"Year of the Dragon" (page
55) but uses fewer fabrics
and makes slight changes in
strip sizes and arrangements.

Phosphorescence

By Marge Edie, 1996, Clemson, South Carolina, 28½" x 43". Underwater landscapes come alive with an otherworldly glow in the right viewing conditions. Cool colors and a range of values set the mood.

Raven Wind

By Marge Edie, 1997, Clemson, South Carolina, 41¼" x 27". I substituted a whole section of fabric for one color run in each tube, so that the Bargello appears to float above the background. Held sideways, I could feel a breeze and see a blackbird flying from the West. You might create a cityscape against a sunset or a wintry sky using the same approach. And you can make two quilts, instead of one, from your color runs!

Autumn Wonder

By Lori Kuba, 1997, Seneca, South Carolina, 32½" x 46½". Lori volunteered her talents to experiment with the "Vermont" structure using a variety of strip widths in her color runs. Varying the strip width allowed her to empha- size favorite fabrics and include smaller amounts of those not as important to the color scheme.

Kansas

By Marge Edie, 1995, Clemson, South Carolina, 24¼" x 33¼". This was my first venture into slant Bargello. It reminded me of grain harvests and storage silos in the Great Plains landscape.

Sweet Dreams

By Susan Kopczyk, 1997, Yorktown, Virginia, 56" x 40". Susan is my Bargello soul sister. I knew that, as with Priscilla Hair, I could turn her loose and the result would be fantastic! Her computer background enables her to explore design possibilities limited only by her imagination. Our roles as teacher and student are now reversed!

Streamers

By Marge Edie, 1997, Clemson, South Carolina, 35" x 51". Using only one set of fabrics removes the dimensionality from the "Crystal City" (page 81) structure, but it is a pleasing alternative. A narrower range of values creates a striped pattern across the quilt.

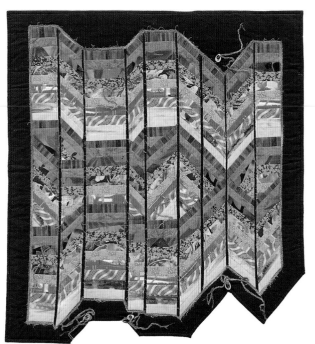

DANCING IN THE SHADOWS

By Priscilla Evans Hair, 1997, Easley, South Carolina, 32" x 35". Priscilla put her design genius to work, using her wonderful instinct for fabric combinations to create this one-of-a-kind quilt. Her creative talent usually flows best without, or in spite of, a traditional framework, so this quilt was a special gift to me and this book. The Bargello units are raw-edge appliquéd onto the navy background with variegated thread.

BLINDED BY THE LIGHT—DAYBREAK ON THE STRAND

By Marge Edie, 1996, Clemson, South Carolina, 27½" x 37¾". I created this piece for the "Smiling Faces, Beautiful Places" quilt competition sponsored by the Anderson County, South Carolina, Arts Center. It combines several variations of traditional Bargello—composite strips, separator strips from three different fabrics, and extension of the design elements into the border—to create a dynamic design.

MEET THE AUTHOR

*M*arge Edie lives in Clemson, South Carolina, and is married to a professor of chemical engineering. She and Dan have lived in Clemson for more than twenty years. Their family includes a daughter and son-in-law, a son and daughter-in-law, and sweet grandchildren. Marge and Dan met at Ohio University, where she earned a Bachelor of Fine Arts degree. She taught art in the Sandusky, Ohio, public schools, did a variety of freelance design work and commissioned painting, and worked as a graphic artist in a printing company. After taking undergraduate and graduate courses in computer science, Marge worked for nearly twelve years in the administrative programming services for Clemson University, developing computer systems for various offices on campus. It was after she "retired" that her quilting habit grew, and her involvement in the geometries of Bargello led to her first book, Bargello Quilts *(That Patchwork Place, 1994). She began to explore the slant possibilities shortly after her first book, and now teaches both traditional and slant Bargello structures around the country.*